SCIENTIFIC
Problem Solving

An Introduction to Technology

by George Mills and John Aitken

Fearon Teacher Aids
Carthage, Illinois

First North American Edition 1989
by Fearon Teacher Aids
1204 Buchanan Street, Carthage, Illinois 62321

Copyright © 1984, 1985 Holmes McDougall Limited; Edinburgh, Scotland. First published as Starting Technology: Books 1 and 2.

ISBN 0-8224-6324-5
Printed in the United States of America

I.9 8 7

INTRODUCTION

A modern curriculum for elementary schools should include some structured treatment of science and technology. The choice of topics should aim to provide a wide and firm base for future scientific studies. The activities should interest both girls and boys and, in a thoroughly practical manner, involve them in solving a wide variety of problems in areas such as design and construction. The activities in *Scientific Problem Solving* aim to fulfill these goals, and to cultivate inquiring and innovative minds.

First published in the UK as two books, this collection of activities is presented here as one volume. David S. Lake Publishers is pleased to be able to present North American teachers with this excellent set of activities. The prime objective of this book is to encourage thoughtful ingenuity. The emphasis on experimentation, design, invention, testing, and research skills fosters a spirit of innovation and problem solving.

We have retained British spellings and usages in both the teacher's notes and on reproducible student pages. Most of these elements are quite self-explanatory. However, below you will find a list of British terms for various materials encountered in the text with a "translation" to more familiar items.

British terms
A4 paper size = 8 1/2 x 11
sticky tape= transparent tape
card=manila,tag, or construction paper
PVA glue= white glue
drawing pins= thumb tacks or push pins
candy floss= popsicle stick or tongue depressor
metre stick= metric ruler
lolly stick=popsicle stick
rubbers= erasers
cotton reel= sewing-thread spool
elastic bands=rubber bands

The present volume is organized into two parts, Level 1 and Level 2. Each has a separate table of contents, and the detailed teacher's notes precede the worksheets for each level.

CONTENTS

Scientific Problem Solving
LEVEL 1

Teacher's notes on the seven topics

TEACHER'S NOTES

1 Instruments

Aims

a To develop awareness of some of the ways in which the Earth's natural resources are located.

b To make a sensitive scientific instrument (magnetometer) and use it in a game of skill to detect hidden 'iron ore'.

c To develop mathematical and mapping skills by using two-dimensional co-ordinates to specify the location of the iron ore deposit.

Procedure

a EARTH SURVEY (1.1) is an information sheet outlining the methods of obtaining satellite data on the Earth's natural resources. The magnetometer (basically a compass) is introduced as one sensitive instrument used in the detection of iron ore. This sheet leads directly to 1.2.

b SIMPLE MAGNETOMETER (1.2) involves the construction and testing of a delicate detecting instrument. A hair is used in preference to a thread because it is a single fibre without twists, and allows the suspended magnetic needle to move freely in response to a magnetic field. The handle is not essential and can be omitted if desired. The magnetometer is needed for the iron ore survey.

c IRON ORE SURVEY (1.3 and 1.4) makes use of the magnetometer to detect a hidden piece of iron. The game demands good co-ordination and gentle movement. The area in question must be scanned in a systematic way. Pupils will become highly skilled with practice, at which stage you could hide two samples, with interesting results!

Notes

a Some background science work may be necessary on magnetism, magnetic substances, and how a compass works (the Earth's magnetism).

b A lesson on the use of the map grid can be given by asking pupils to place coins on the topographical details, and name the co-ordinates (B—9: volcano, and so on).

Follow-up work

Issue Research Sheets and ask pupils to use reference books to list, with simple labelled drawings, instruments used in Earth survey work (e.g. weather instruments, geiger counters, seismic recorders).

Materials (for each pupil)

SIMPLE MAGNETOMETER	IRON ORE SURVEY
Sheet 1.2	Sheets 1.3 and 1.4
bar magnet (shared)	blank A4 sheet of card
hair or thread	magnetometer (assembled)
paper clip	scissors
scissors	sticky tape
small needle	thin pieces of iron (food can)/washers
sticky tape	

2 Hinges and Valves

Aims

a To assemble and test variations on a simple mechanism — the hinge — and to improve the designs by experiment.

b To extend the hinge concept to the understanding of valve systems.

c To introduce the use of symbols in design work.

Procedure

a HINGE DESIGNS (2.1 and 2.2) should be issued with the necessary materials and designs 1 and 2 discussed. Pupils can then make up the designs and test them.

b Pupils should try to design simple feasible hinges for design 3, to link R with S, using paper clips only. Encourage construction and testing of their designs. Modify the hinges on further Design Sheets if necessary.

c Issue the HINGE PROBLEM (2.3) with the necessary materials, including X and Y from sheet 2.2. Aim for a good working hinge from each pupil.

d Discuss the possibilities of the use as valves of the 'one-way systems' they have made. This sheet leads directly to 2.4.

e ONE-WAY TRAFFIC (2.4) can now be issued. Aim for a good working model valve from each pupil.

f VALVE DRAWINGS (2.5) should be worked through with the class. Questions 5 and 6 can be demonstrated or left for home research, as you see fit.

g VALVE PROBLEMS (2.6 and 2.7) are ideal for consolidation of the concept, and interpretation of symbols.

Follow-up work

As work on this topic progresses, pupils will encounter a number of applications of hinges and valves. It is important to continue observation and interpretation of these devices for some time.

Materials (for each pupil)

HINGE DESIGNS
Sheets 2.1, 2.2 and 2.3
Design Sheet
paper clips
plastic straws
plasticine
scissors
soft wire
sticky tape
wire snips

VALVE DESIGNS
Sheet 2.4
Research Sheet
marbles
plastic straws
plasticine
ruler
scissors
sheet of card
small box lid or tray
soft wire
stapler
sticky tape
wire snips

3 Sorting

Aims

a To explore some properties of materials (iron, wood, glass, copper, etc.) by separating samples.

b To encourage creative design, testing and manipulation of equipment.

c To develop the ability to interpret machine drawings and predict function.

Procedure

a SORTING MATERIALS (3.1) asks pupils to separate manually four types of materials from the assortment given, using the evidence of their hands and eyes, and record the results in a table. Help with the names of materials and properties may be necessary, e.g. copper/heavy, glass/smooth.

b Pupils are then asked to design a machine to sort the items. Allow a variety of ideas, for instance weight, shape, volume — and try to discuss individual suggestions. Some children perform poorly at this stage — if so move on to sheet 3.2.

c The AUTOMATIC SORTING MACHINE (3.2) should be issued and discussed in a general way. Pupils may be able to suggest what it is for, having done sheet 3.1.

d Focus their attention on the properties of the materials to be sorted. The machine is crude in operation but has the vital feature that items are not sorted manually. The magnet attracts the paper clips; the marbles roll down to the plasticine barrier; while tilting the lid allows the coins and wood to fall into the water where they are separated.

e AN INTERESTING FIND! (3.3 and 3.4) can be used before or after the first two sheets, or as a lesson in its own right. Issue both sheets and ask what the machine could be used for. Pupils should try to visualise the plan made up in three dimensions, as in the drawing. Do not mention coins at this stage. When pupils have assembled their own machines, some of them may have ideas as to the function.

f Bring coins out to test the machines. No accurate sizes have been given for the slots through which the coins drop, to avoid giving too much away, so adjustment of the plastic straws will be necessary.

g Pupils should devise a table of results on a Research Sheet — e.g. how many coins of each size were correctly sorted in ten trials; what went wrong (defects in machine); etc.

Notes

The simple nature of the materials used will result in some problems of operation. For instance, blobs of glue on the coin sorting machine will prevent coins from rolling down smoothly. Avoid this by demonstrating how to spread the glue carefully with a matchstick, and warn pupils to keep it off their hands and clothes.

Follow-up work

a Suitable follow-up work will enable pupils to appreciate that machines which work to finer tolerances, using plastics and metals, are much more accurate and smooth in operation. Examine some machines in detail, such as scales, sewing machine, or whatever is easily available.

b Try designing and constructing a machine which sorts out different-sized balls (marbles, beads, peas, etc.). Or various mixtures of materials can be tested (iron dust and brass dust sorted by magnet, for example).

Materials (for each pupil)

SORTING MATERIALS
Sheet 3.1
Design Sheet
coins
marbles
paper clips
small wood blocks

AN INTERESTING FIND!
Sheets 3.3 and 3.4
Research Sheet
empty matchboxes
jar lid
millimetre ruler
plastic straws
PVA glue
scissors   selection of coins or washers with three
sticky tape   different diameters

AUTOMATIC SORTING MACHINE (for class or groups)
Sheet 3.2 for each pupil
Design Sheet for each pupil
items as used for sheet 3.1
pencil
plasticine
round pencil
scissors
shoe box
sticky tape
strong magnet (horseshoe or bar)
tray of water

4 Robots

Aims

a To develop an awareness of robotic controls and devices used in industrial operations.

b To construct and use a simple model capable of spatial operations (three-dimensional movement and electromagnetic lifting).

c To develop co-ordination skills by performing a set of operations against the clock.

d To introduce the idea of power control from a distance using air (simple pneumatics) and water (simple hydraulics) to work the robot arm.

Procedure

a   ROBOTS (4.1) is an information sheet on robots and their control systems. The aim is to dispel the idea that scientific and industrial robots look like people. Robots must be seen as devices which can perform simple or complex operations, following human instructions. They can sometimes speak, see, and even think, according to how they have been programmed.

b   The POP-UP ROBOT (4.2) is a simple toy which can easily be made, but it is a vital first experience in solving later problems associated with operating a robot. The pivot, the lever and pneumatic operation all feature in this activity.

c   OPERATING A ROBOT (4.3 and 4.4) involves constructing a model industrial robot for use in lifting pieces of iron in a 'factory' and moving them to another location for 'processing'.

d   Issue the sheets with the necessary materials and aim for a good working model from each pupil. Colouring the card cut-out with felt pens adds to the effect.

e   PNEUMATIC OPERATION PROBLEM (4.5) introduces the problem of working the robot at a distance. The electrical connections can easily be extended and a simple switch made to turn the electromagnet on and off. Moving the robot arm by air is rather more difficult, but some children will remember the principle of blowing into a bag from sheet 4.2. Allow them a variety of items to work with, including balloons, pump, syringes, plastic bags and tubing, plus anything else from the list below.

f   The solution given on sheet 4.5 gives the idea that blowing up a bag can be a way of exerting force at a distance. It is therefore best to issue this part of the sheet separately, after pupils have tried to devise their own solutions. Of course, many other methods of moving the robot arm by air may be suggested.

g   HYDRAULIC OPERATION PROBLEM (4.6) moves on to substitute water for air as a means of operating the robot arm. Issue this sheet only after pupils have had a reasonable attempt at designing an air control system.

h   The two-syringe system, once filled with water, can readily be connected so that one piston is fixed to the robot arm and is driven by the other piston (out and in) from a distance. Warn pupils not to pull the operating piston right out of the syringe.

Notes

a   The principles of electromagnetism could be covered by a simple demonstration.

b   If contact is held for too long a period the battery will quickly drain. Allow pupils one try each (for a minute) in the first instance, and have a spare battery available. They can take the models home and practise.

c   Pupils should find that hydraulic operation is much superior to the pneumatic system. Unlike gases, liquids cannot be compressed. The force transmitted is therefore much greater and no mechanism (the elastic) is required to allow the arm to return quickly.

Follow-up work

a   Issue Research Sheets and ask pupils to use reference books or magazines to find examples of automation — robots in use in recent years, giving dates, countries, process used for, etc.

b   Ask groups to design another magnetic machine and 'programme' it to carry out a different set of tasks.

c   Vehicle braking systems could be studied for examples of pneumatics and hydraulics.

Materials

POP-UP ROBOT (for groups)
Sheet 4.2
card (thick and thin pieces)
cardboard box
drawing pins (large and small)
glue

plastic bags
plastic tubing
sticky tape
thin stick (candy floss)
thread or thin string

OPERATING A ROBOT
(for each pupil)
Sheets 4.3 and 4.4
paper fastener
scissors
small iron nail
sticky tape
1½m thin bell wire
   (plastic-covered copper wire)
(for class or groups)
4½ V battery
metre stick or tape
minute timer
paper clips
plastic tub

PNEUMATICS AND HYDRAULICS **(for groups)**
Sheets 4.5 and 4.6
balloons
basin of water
bicycle or balloon pump
card (A4 sheets)
elastic bands
extra bell wire
paper clips
plastic bags
plastic syringes
plastic tubing
sticky tape
thread or thin string

5 Bridges

Aims

a To develop problem-solving skills through creative design, practical ingenuity, simple experimental procedure and recording of results.

b To increase understanding of some reasons for structural design, and encourage observation of the environment.

Procedure

a BRIDGE PROBLEM (5.1 and 5.2) where the aim is to design and build a bridge using the materials provided, which must support at least 100 g weight. The river outline is needed for sheets 5.3 and 5.4.

b BEAM SHAPES (5.3 and 5.4) give a systematic analysis of beam shapes for two paper 'plates' of the same area.

c Pupils' tests should establish that strength and rigidity are best achieved when the plates are bent or folded. Tubes or angled beams give the strongest structures — flat plates are weakest. Also, when two or more beams are 'keyed' together the structure has added strength and rigidity.

Notes

a Pupils can return to the bridge problem when they have tested different beam shapes. Their performance should be much better. Over 100 g weight can be supported on a well-designed bridge.

b Possible beam designs are:

Follow-up work

a Suggest that pupils use rolled newspapers to build a beam bridge across two chairs, strong enough to support a child.

b Look at bridges in your locality, especially beam bridges. This could lead to a class project, using Research Sheets, drawings and paintings for display.

Materials (for each pupil)

BRIDGE PROBLEM
Sheets 5.1 and 5.2
Design Sheet
empty matchboxes
100 g plasticine
   (divided into 10 equal weights)
scissors

BEAM SHAPES
Sheets 5.3 and 5.4
river crossing assembly
100 g plasticine
   (divided into 10 equal weights)
scissors

6 Frameworks

Aims

a To reinforce and extend understanding of structural shapes, by establishing that triangulation gives rigidity and strength to a framework, with minimum use of material.

b To extend the work done on bridges in developing problem-solving skills through experimental procedure and recording of results.

Procedure

a FRAMEWORKS (6.1) is an information sheet showing a variety of modern structures. Pupils will appreciate from their work on bridges and beams that L girders, H beams, tubes, etc. are stronger than flat plates.

b The examples show that these beams are held together in frameworks which depend on cross-beams (triangulation) for rigidity and strength. The information sheet can be issued before or after the others in this topic.

c TOWER PROBLEM (6.2) introduces the idea of a tower structure and poses the problem of building the highest possible tower, using only ten pipecleaners as beams, which will support 100 g.

d The most economical way of combining maximum height and strength is to build a tripod with cross-beams, as shown. Many other designs are possible. The cross-struts are commonly omitted at this stage, so aim to have pupils discover this for themselves. If results are poor, move on to sheet 6.3.

e SIMPLE FRAMEWORKS (6.3) reinforces the fact that triangulation gives rigidity, and that the strengthening strips need not join the corners. Aim to have pupils analyse the results in detail.

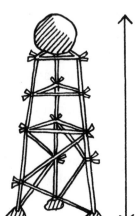

height

Notes

a Make sure all pupils are agreed on how the height of the tower is to be measured — some may shape the plasticine to give more height.

b Pupils can return to the tower problem when they have tested different framework shapes. Results should be much better.

Follow-up work

a   The concept that triangulation gives a strong structure with minimum use of material is of fundamental importance. Mathematical work can be introduced with different triangles, and three-dimensional structures.

b   Look at structures in nature, using Research Sheets to make labelled drawings of leaves, webs, stem formation, etc.

Materials (for each pupil)

TOWER PROBLEM
Sheet 6.2
Design Sheet
millimetre ruler
pipecleaners
plasticine
   (100 g and some spare)
scissors

SIMPLE FRAMEWORKS
Sheet 6.3
Research Sheet
pipecleaners
scissors

7   Propellers

Aims

a   To give a simple introduction to design and testing.

b   To give experience of the designing, testing and development of one application of the propeller, i.e. a powered boat.

Procedure

a   Issue PROPELLER TESTING sheets (7.1 and 7.2) with the necessary materials and discuss the testing of the propeller designs. Encourage pupils to use Design Sheets for further work.

b   POWER BOAT (7.3) involves the construction of a propeller-driven model boat. The work is best done in groups. It is important to have as large a test tank as possible.

Follow-up work

a   The best extension work comes from development of the boat. Different hull shapes, arrangements of ballast, different engine designs and engine arrangement (e.g. twin engines) are all rich areas for 'research and development' and should be actively encouraged.

b   Ask pupils to look up reference books and magazines to find other uses of propellers, and record their findings on Research Sheets.

Materials

PROPELLER TESTING (for each pupil)
Sheets 7.1 and 7.2
cuphook/drawing pins
darning needle
plastic straw
plasticine
scissors
strong thread

POWER BOAT (for groups)
Sheet 7.3
bead
crayons
elastic bands
empty pen tube
paper clip
plastic bottle
plastic straw
plasticine
scissors
small piece card
sticky tape
thin wire

1. The Earth's crust contains many valuable materials used in industry, such as oil, iron ore, and other minerals. As supplies are used up, it becomes important to find new sources.

solar panel

antenna

cameras

{instrument package

magnetometer

2. Earth Resource Satellites send back information from space which helps scientists to locate new deposits of natural resources. The satellites also send back data on the weather (drought or flood areas), pollution, forest fires, etc.

3. Satellite information on mineral deposits is checked in a ground survey, by testing the area with special instruments. You must make sure that the correct place has been found before any mining starts.

MAGNETOMETER

DIAL

4. You are going to do the same kind of test, using a sensitive instrument called a magnetometer. Special types of magnetometers are fitted in satellites which are used to detect hidden iron deposits on Earth.

5. Begin by constructing your own magnetometer, using sheet 1.2. Then organise a survey of Mystery Island using sheets 1.3 and 1.4.

1.2 SIMPLE MAGNETOMETER

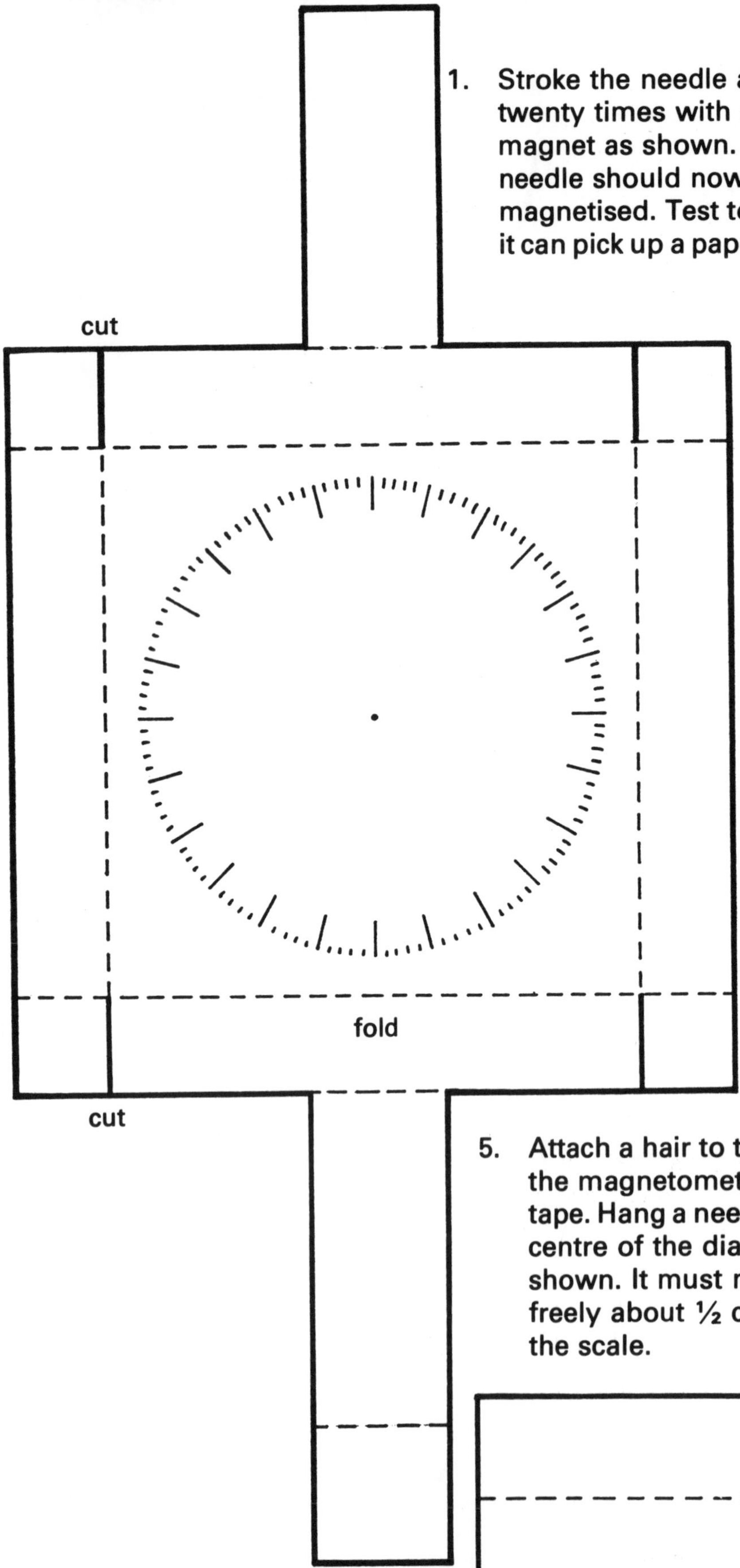

1. Stroke the needle about twenty times with a magnet as shown. Your needle should now be magnetised. Test to see if it can pick up a paper clip.

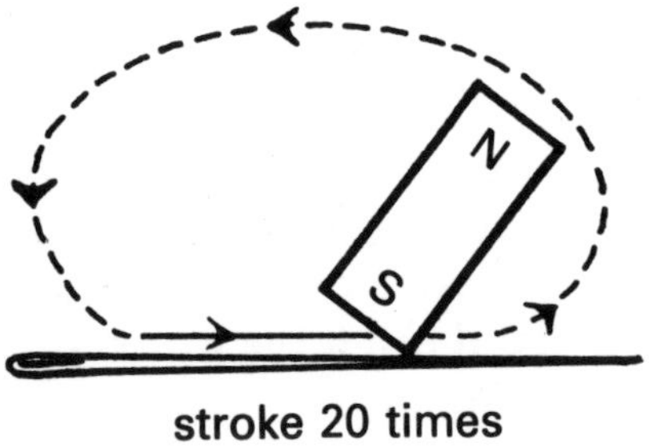

stroke 20 times

cut

cut

fold

2. Cut out the magnetometer, along the solid lines. (The dotted lines are for folding.)

3. Fold and tape it as shown.

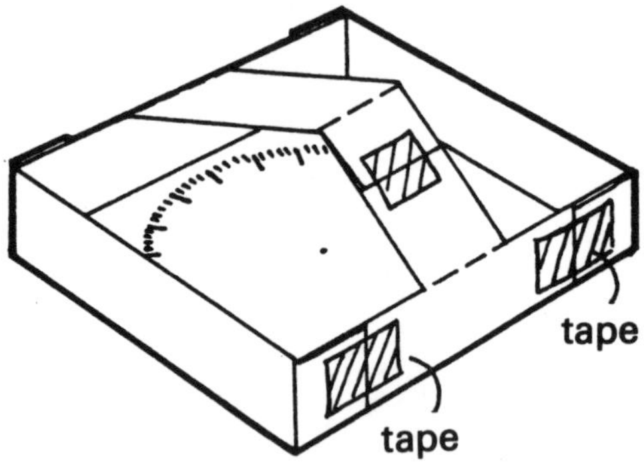

tape

tape

4. Cut out the handle and tape it to a corner.

5. Attach a hair to the top of the magnetometer with tape. Hang a needle at the centre of the dial, as shown. It must move freely about ½ cm above the scale.

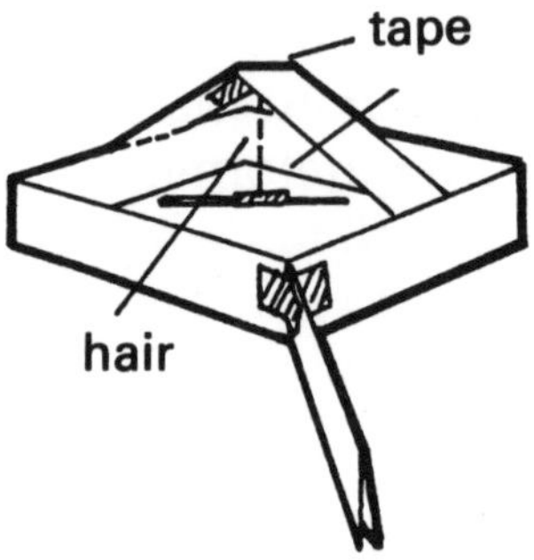

tape

hair

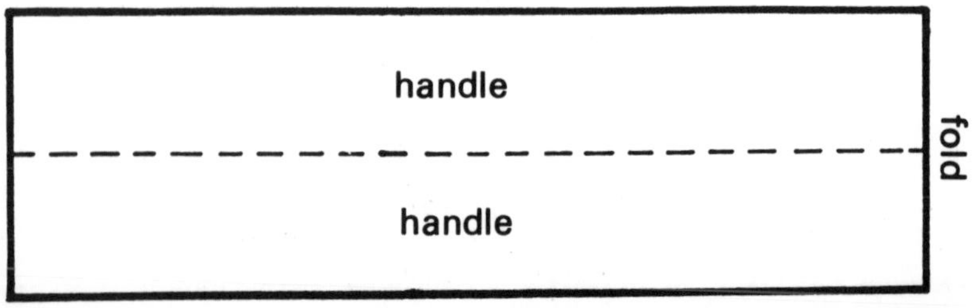

handle

handle

fold

PRINT ON CARD

1.3 IRON ORE SURVEY

1. Ask a friend to tape a thin piece of iron underneath the map of Mystery Island. This is the iron ore deposit which you must locate. You must not see where the iron is fixed. Your friend should tape a blank card to the map card as shown, to hide the position of the deposit.

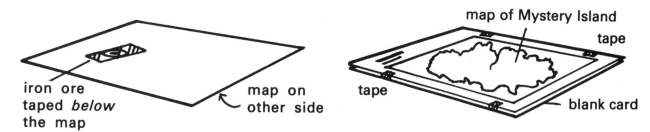

iron ore taped *below* the map

map on other side

map of Mystery Island

tape

tape

blank card

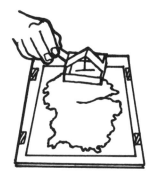

2. Use your magnetometer to survey the island. Can you locate the iron ore deposit? Mark the location with a cross. Better still, note the co-ordinates of the square where the deposit is.

3. Remember to move your magnetometer gently and slowly over the area. The needle will point towards the iron ore when you are near it.

4. Make sure that you check the complete area — perhaps there is another deposit hidden?

5. Play a survey game with friends and keep a score.

name	actual position of iron ore	position found by magnetometer	points score exact = 3 near = 1 miss = 0
Tom	F—3	C—11	0

1.4 IRON ORE SURVEY   Surveyor _____

Mystery Island

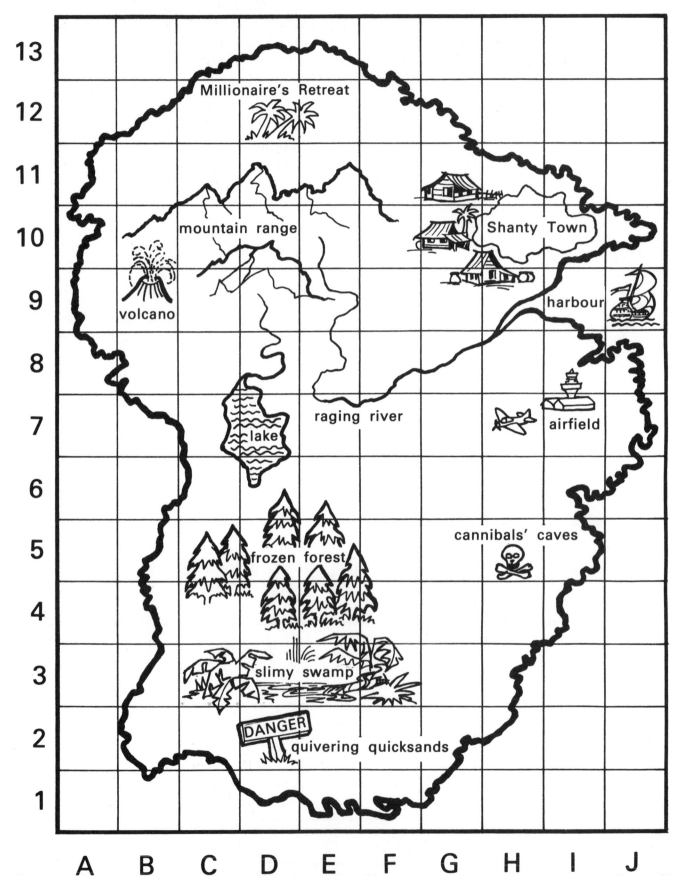

Millionaire's Retreat

mountain range

volcano

Shanty Town

harbour

raging river

airfield

lake

frozen forest

cannibals' caves

slimy swamp

DANGER

quivering quicksands

13 12 11 10 9 8 7 6 5 4 3 2 1

A B C D E F G H I J

PRINT ON CARD

2.1 HINGE DESIGNS Design tester _____

DESIGN 1

1. Cut out shapes A and B from the hinge designs on sheet 2.2.

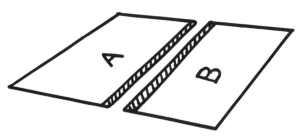

2. Tape the two shaded edges together as shown, to make a simple hinge.

3. Test the hinge by bending it backwards and forwards. Does it move easily?

DESIGN 2

4. Cut out shapes P and Q. Tape a plastic straw to the shaded edge of P.

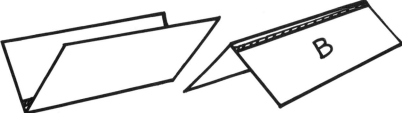

5. Push a length of wire through the straw, as shown.

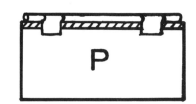

6. Bend the ends of the wire round, and tape them to the edge of Q.

7. Test the hinge as before. Does it work better than design 1?

DESIGN 3

8. Cut out shapes R and S. You have to design a hinge using these two pieces and paper clips —*nothing else.* You can bend the clips to any shape. Draw your ideas on a Design Sheet, and discuss them with friends.

9. Make the hinge to your design and test it. Can it be improved? Try, and test again.

Name _____

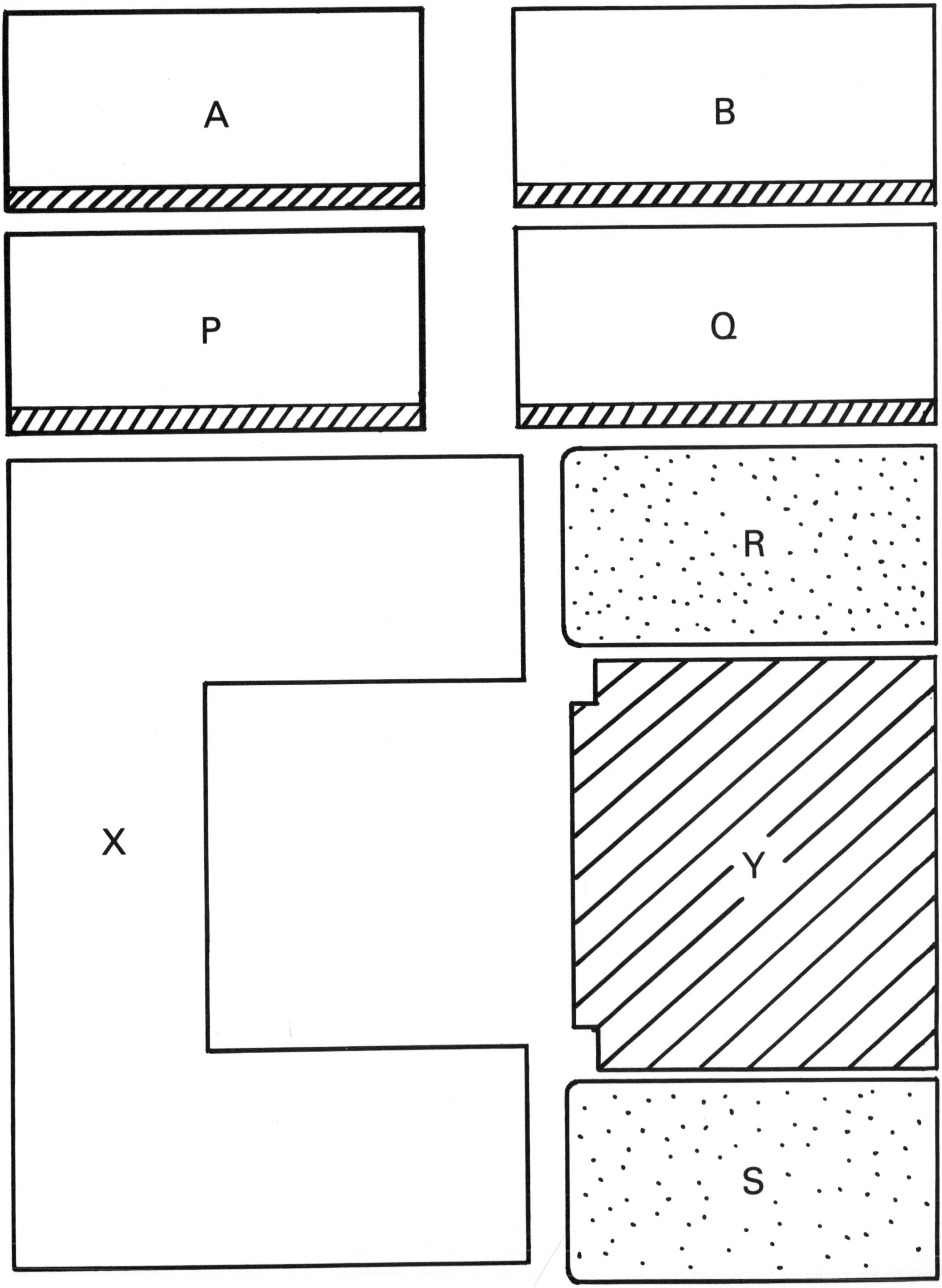

A

B

P

Q

R

X

Y

S

PRINT ON CARD

2.3 HINGE PROBLEM Engineer _____

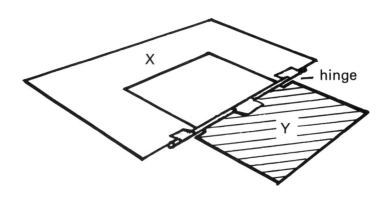

1. Cut out shapes X and Y from the hinge designs on sheet 2.2. Can you make a hinge so that the two pieces are joined like this?

2. Test your hinge to see if Y moves freely and easily.

3. Here are two suggestions for designing this hinge, which you could try. Test them to find out which works best.

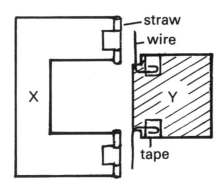
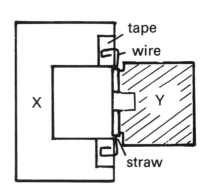

4. When you are satisfied with your hinge, fix it upright on the desk with plasticine as shown:

Part Y will hang down like a door.

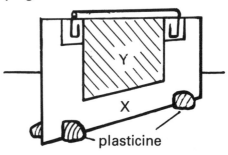

5. Gently push a finger through the door. If you push from one side, the door opens.

If you push from the other side, it stays closed!

6. It is a one-way system. You have made a VALVE.
   A valve is a structure that only lets things through from one direction.

2.4 ONE-WAY TRAFFIC Technologist _____

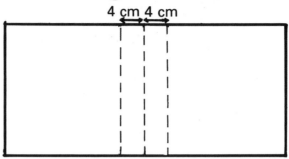

1. On a sheet of card which fits neatly inside your box lid or tray, rule three lines 4 cm apart.

2. Bend the sheet as shown.

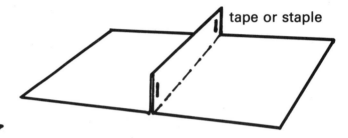

3. Tape or staple the fold at either end.

4. Cut a square hole in the fold.

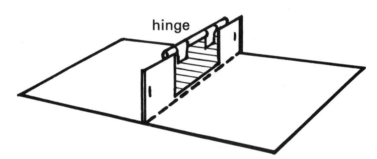

5. Cut a piece of card a little larger than the hole you have made. Using your best hinge design, fix the card to hang down like a flap. This should now be a one-way system — a valve.

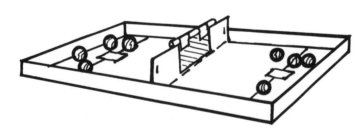

6. Tape your valve inside the box lid or tray. Put three or four marbles at both ends.

7. Tilt the lid backwards and forwards. Watch the marbles carefully. Can you explain what happens to them?

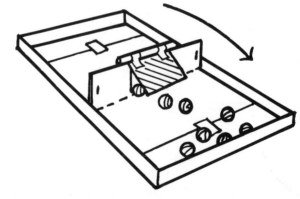

2.5 VALVE DRAWINGS

1. A valve only lets things flow through from one direction.

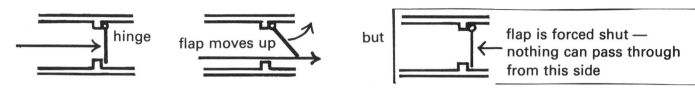

2. Here are two valves. Draw an arrow on each to show which way they allow movement.

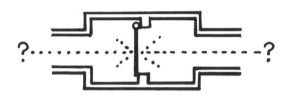

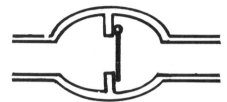

3. ## ANOTHER TYPE OF VALVE

Flaps A and B can be pushed open

in this direction . . .

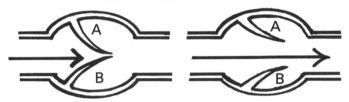

This type of valve is found in your veins.

. . . but not in this direction.

The flaps are forced shut and prevent anything flowing through, so it is a one-way system.

4. ## A BALL VALVE

The ball can be pushed out of the way.

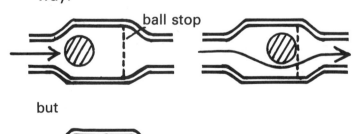

but

5. Use reference books to find another type of valve. Make a labelled drawing on a Research Sheet. List other things that have valves underneath your drawing.

6. Open a pump to see what kind of valve it has.

When flow is from the other direction, the ball is jammed firmly into a narrow space. This prevents anything from passing through.

2.6 VALVE PROBLEM 1

Name _____

1. With a pencil, trace a path through this maze of pipes and valves. Start at X and end at Y.

2. You must not cross any lines, or go through a valve the wrong way.

3. Each time you come to a valve, remember that you can only go through it in one direction.

1. Three dangerous liquids are being pumped into a mixing chamber. The mixture must then flow down pipe X. It must not be allowed to flow back into pipes A, B or C or there would be the risk of an explosion.

2. Liquid 4 must flow down pipe Y to join the mixture. The mixture must not be allowed to reach the liquid 4 storage chamber.

3. Valves are needed to make sure that the various liquids flow in the correct directions. Draw in the valves that you think will be necessary.

4. Use the symbol ⊶ in exactly the right places. (See sheet 2.5.)

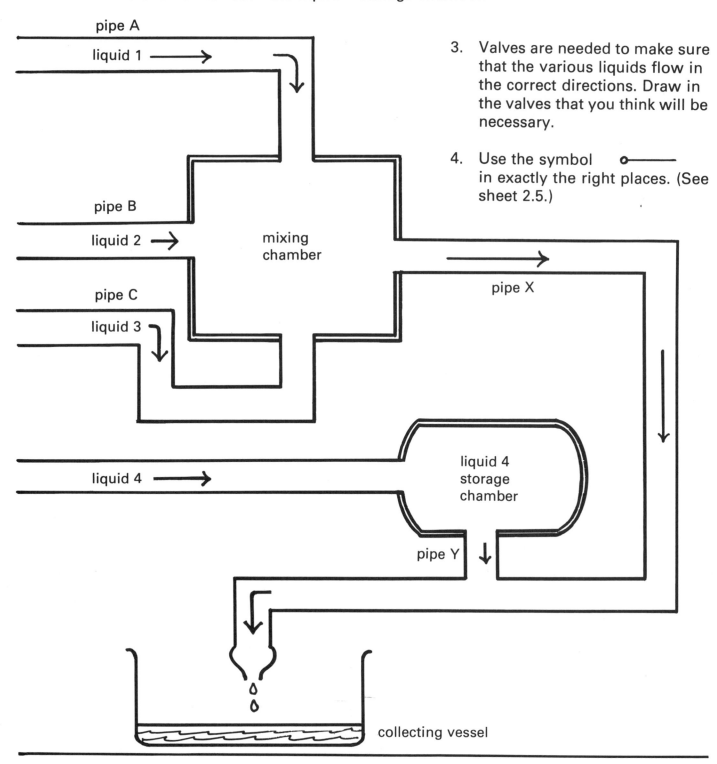

3.1 SORTING MATERIALS

1. You have been given lots of items made of different materials.

2. Sort them out carefully. Complete the table of results. One is partly done for you.

	name of item	What is it made of?	number counted	special features of the item
1	block	wood		cube-shaped hard
2				
3				
4				

3. It·was easy to sort out big pieces like these, using your eyes and hands. What would happen if the pieces were tiny, or if they all looked the same? Some pieces might be wood, and some glass, and you couldn't tell. How would you sort them? Scientists have to solve this problem by designing special machines. They can sort materials dug from the earth, for instance soil samples, to find out what they contain.

4. Try to think of a way to sort your items again, without lifting them out of the pile one at a time. Use a Design Sheet to draw or write down your ideas for a sorting machine. You can ask your teacher for any simple item you need to try out your ideas.

Miss! Please may I have a computer?

No!

3.2 AUTOMATIC SORTING MACHINE

1. The drawing shows Sam's machine for sorting out different materials. Look at it carefully and see if you can understand how it works.

SAM'S MACHINE

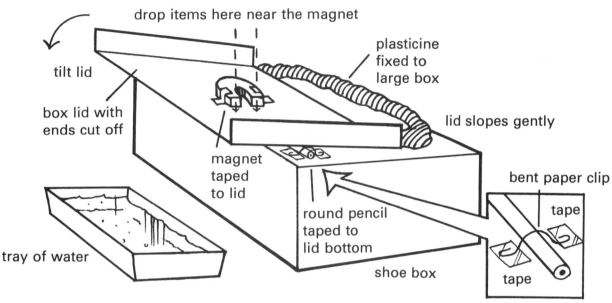

drop items here near the magnet

tilt lid

plasticine fixed to large box

box lid with ends cut off

lid slopes gently

magnet taped to lid

bent paper clip

tape

tray of water

round pencil taped to lid bottom

shoe box

tape

2. Explain below how the machine would separate coins, marbles, paper clips, and wood blocks.

_____

_____

_____

_____

_____

3. Try to make a group model of the machine and test it. Can you improve on the design? Draw or write down your ideas on a Design Sheet.

I need to think first!

3.3 AN INTERESTING FIND!

Technologist _____

1. While cleaning out an old desk a teacher found this torn drawing, and a plan of a machine. The name of the machine was missing, so she didn't know what it was used for. What do you think? How does it work?

2. If you can't guess from the drawing on this sheet, build the machine from the plan on sheet 3.4, then think about it. How can you test it? Your teacher will help you if necessary.

3. Use a Research Sheet to explain your ideas, how you made the machine, and how you tested it. Include the results of your tests.

Plan for a ⌒ machine

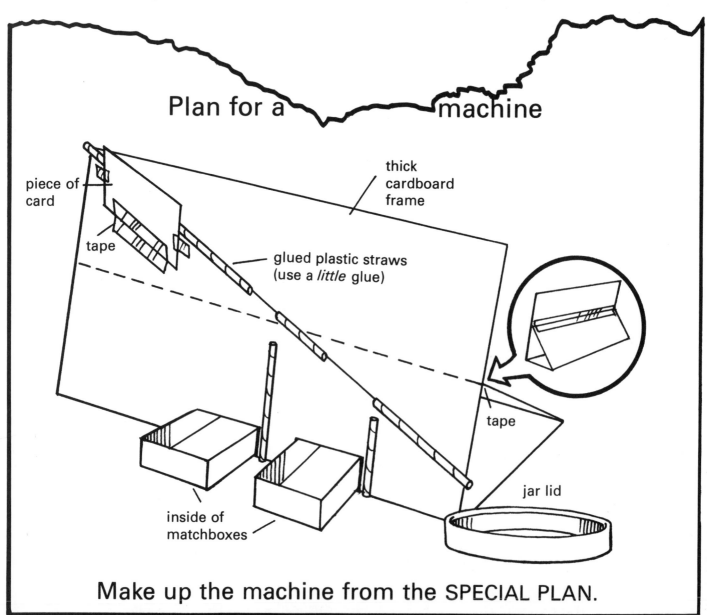

piece of card

thick cardboard frame

tape

glued plastic straws (use a *little* glue)

tape

jar lid

inside of matchboxes

Make up the machine from the SPECIAL PLAN.

3.4 AN INTERESTING FIND!

Name ______________________

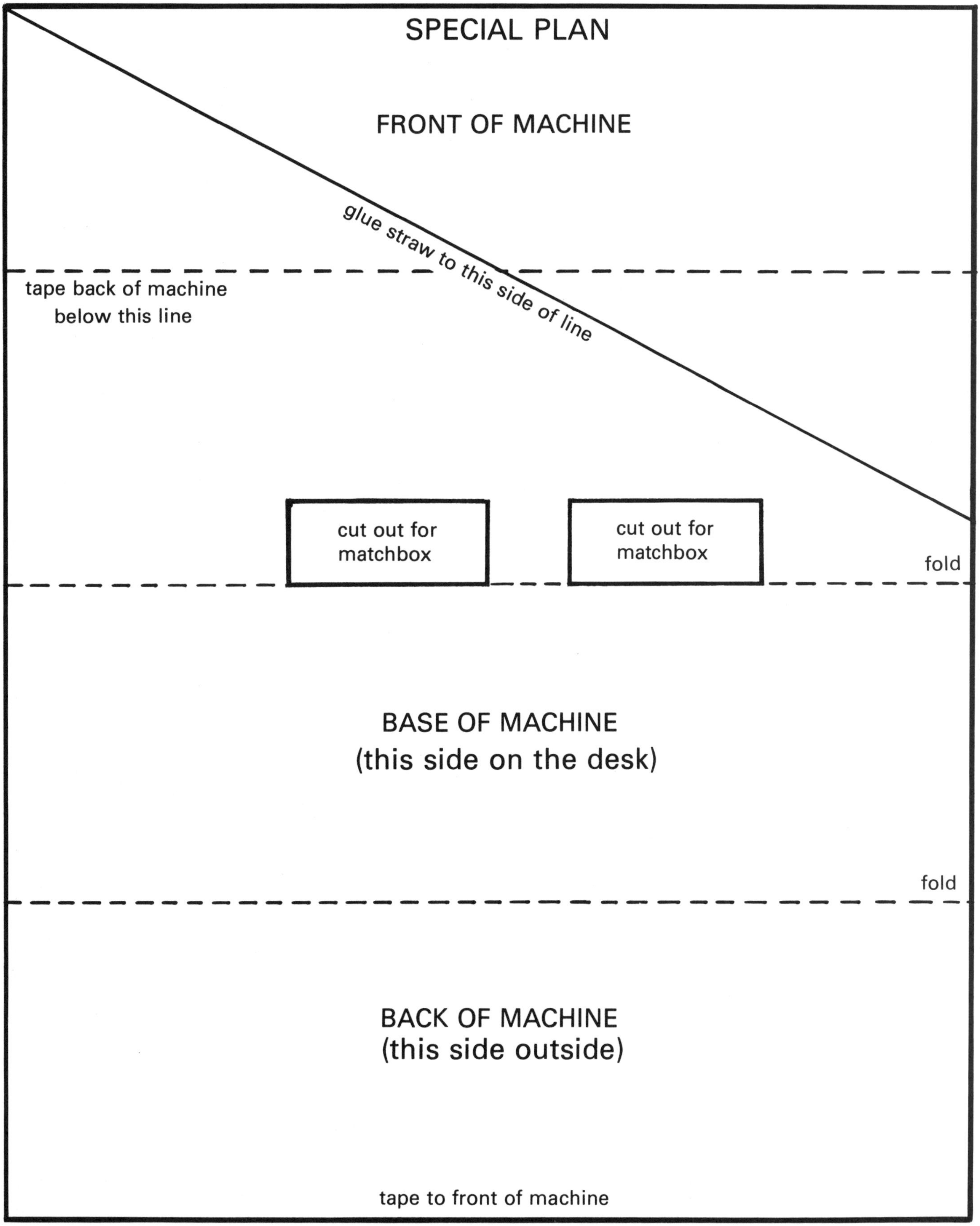
SPECIAL PLAN
FRONT OF MACHINE
glue straw to this side of line
tape back of machine below this line
cut out for matchbox
cut out for matchbox
fold
BASE OF MACHINE
(this side on the desk)
fold
BACK OF MACHINE
(this side outside)
tape to front of machine

PRINT ON THICK CARD

4.1 ROBOTS

Name _____

1. You may think that all robots look something like this! But there are many kinds of robots in use today which are nothing like 'metal monsters'.

2. Robots work on space satellites and in factories, doing work that would be very dangerous or very boring for people to do. They can go into space, under the sea, or work in great heat or cold. They can work non-stop without life support systems — air, water, or food — unless they break down, of course!

3. Modern factories can be run almost completely by robots. Some work on production lines, as in a car factory. Others pack and store the finished articles, as in food factories.

4. How does a robot know its job? Skilled scientists have programmed its 'brain'. They do this by instructing a computer how to do the job required. Technicians and engineers are needed as well, to check and maintain the robot's parts.

4.2 POP-UP ROBOT

Name _____

1. The drawing shows a pop-up robot which is controlled by air. Your teacher will give you the necessary materials to make a similar model.

2. Try to make it work so that the robot disappears completely behind the box, then reappears when you blow up the bag. Use either of the cut-out figures below, or try them both at once.

POP-UP ROBOT USING AIR CONTROL

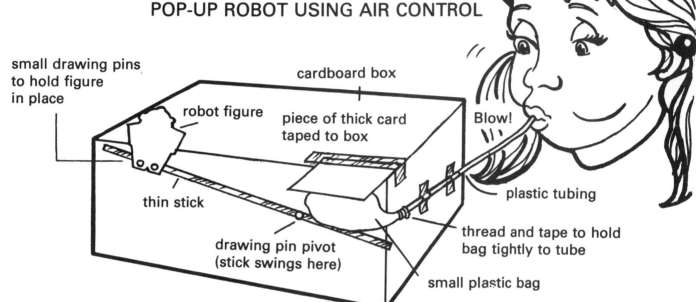

small drawing pins to hold figure in place

cardboard box

robot figure

piece of thick card taped to box

Blow!

thin stick

plastic tubing

drawing pin pivot (stick swings here)

thread and tape to hold bag tightly to tube

small plastic bag

3. Why is the position of the pivot important? See if you can improve on the design. Draw or write down your ideas on a Design Sheet and test them.

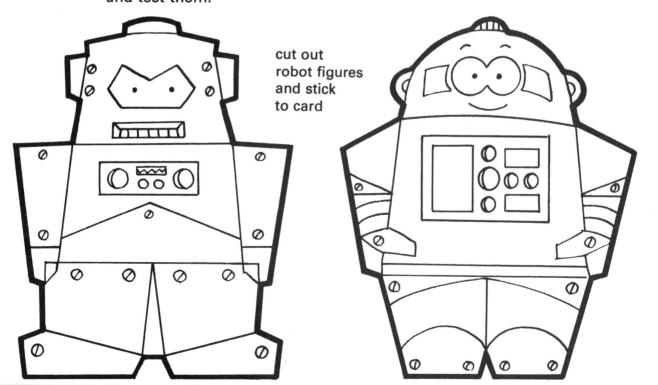

cut out robot figures and stick to card

4.3 OPERATING A ROBOT

1. You are a computer programmer. You have to tell an industrial robot what to do in order to move a load of iron across a factory floor.

2. The robot has been for repairs. You will have to assemble the parts to get it working again. Use the plan on sheet 4.4 as follows:

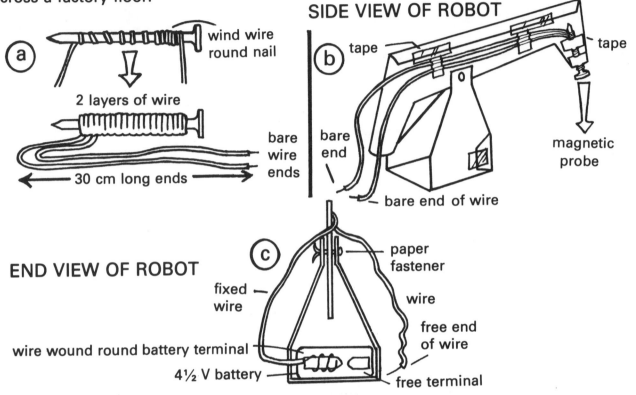

a) wind wire round nail

2 layers of wire

bare wire ends

30 cm long ends

SIDE VIEW OF ROBOT

b) tape

tape

bare end

bare end of wire

magnetic probe

END VIEW OF ROBOT

c) paper fastener

fixed wire

wire

free end of wire

wire wound round battery terminal

4½ V battery

free terminal

3. When you touch the loose wire to the free battery terminal, the robot arm becomes magnetised. The probe will now attract iron, so will pick up the paper clips.

4. If you take the wire away from the battery terminal, the clips will fall off, as the probe is no longer a magnet.

5. The programme for the robot's job is:
   time allowed .... one minute
   task............................. move clips from desk to tub
   distance .... fifty centimetres.

6. Pretend to be the robot's computer brain and control it. How well does it perform? Keep a record of the number of clips moved in one minute. Challenge a friend to do better!

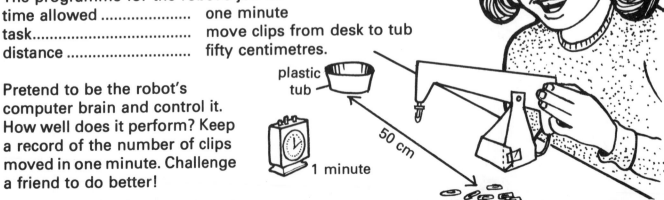

plastic tub

50 cm

1 minute

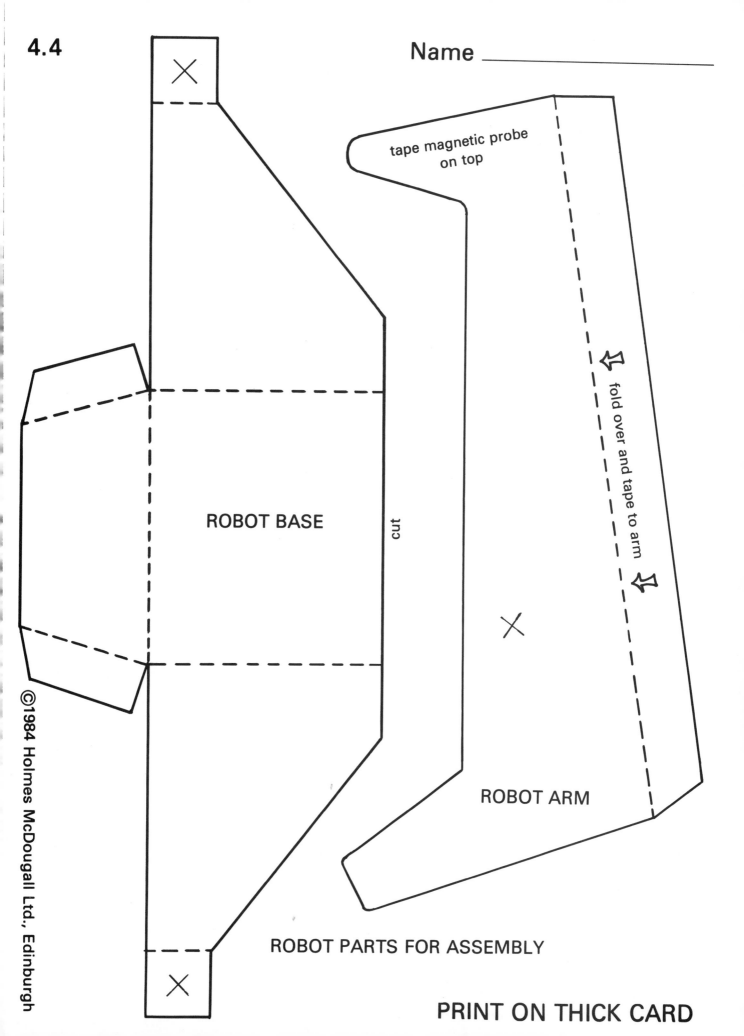

4.4

tape magnetic probe on top

fold over and tape to arm

ROBOT BASE

cut

ROBOT ARM

ROBOT PARTS FOR ASSEMBLY

PRINT ON THICK CARD

4.5 PNEUMATIC OPERATION PROBLEM

1. Pretend that your robot has to work with dangerous materials (such as radio-active substances). You must control it at a distance to avoid contamination.

2. Tape the robot to one end of a sheet of card, and fit the controls to the other end.

3. Fit two controls:

   a Magnetic probe control — make a simple switch, as shown, to control the flow of electricity.

   b Robot arm control — devise a system *using air* which makes the arm move up and down.

   Your teacher will give you various items to help you.

Making things work using air is called PNEUMATIC OPERATION.

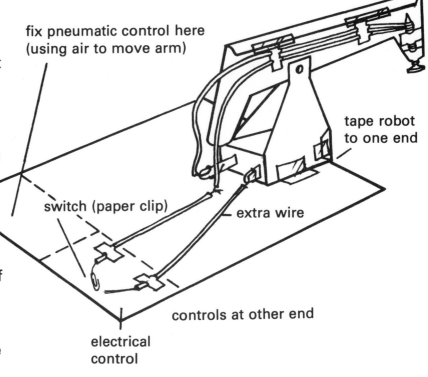

fix pneumatic control here (using air to move arm)

tape robot to one end

switch (paper clip)

extra wire

controls at other end

electrical control

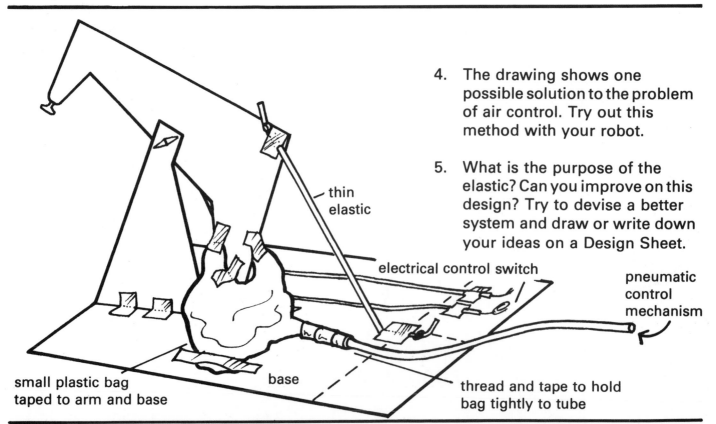

4. The drawing shows one possible solution to the problem of air control. Try out this method with your robot.

5. What is the purpose of the elastic? Can you improve on this design? Try to devise a better system and draw or write down your ideas on a Design Sheet.

thin elastic

electrical control switch

pneumatic control mechanism

small plastic bag taped to arm and base

base

thread and tape to hold bag tightly to tube

4.6 HYDRAULIC OPERATION PROBLEM

1. Instead of using air to operate the robot arm, you have to use water. Using water to transmit forces is called HYDRAULIC OPERATION.

    One way of making a hydraulic system is shown below.

2. Join two plastic syringes with a piece of tubing.

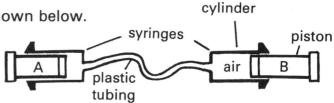

3. Fill the system with water. It is important to avoid getting any air bubbles inside. You can best do this by filling it *under water*, as shown.

4. Take out the hydraulic system and put it on the desk. It should not leak. Push in piston A and observe B. Then push in piston B and observe A. What happens? What would happen if there was air in the system?

5. Fit the hydraulic control to operate your robot arm. One possible solution to the problem is shown in the drawing. Perhaps you can think of a better way? Use a Design Sheet to explain your ideas.

6. How does hydraulic operation compare to pneumatic operation?

5.1 BRIDGE PROBLEM   Engineer _____

1. You have been asked to design and build a beam bridge across this river. It must be strong enough to support *at least* 100 g weight.

2. Look at the river outline on sheet 5.2. You can use up to three steel plates to make beams to bridge the gap.

3. Cut out the steel plates. Set a matchbox on either side of the river, as supports for your bridge.

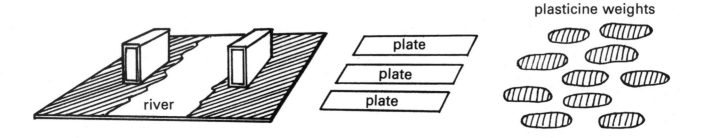

river

plate
plate
plate

plasticine weights

4. Draw a plan of your bridge on a Design Sheet. Remember you can only use up to three plates, made into beams of any shape you like.

5. Build the bridge to your plan. Test it by placing a plasticine weight at the centre, as shown. If it does not collapse, add weights until it does. Note the weight to cause collapse.

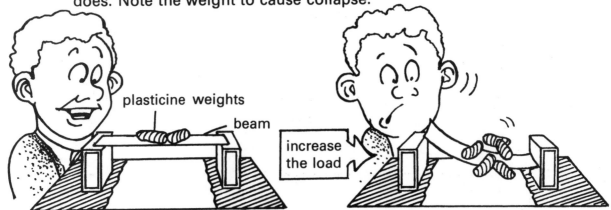

plasticine weights

beam

increase the load

6. Improve your design until the bridge will support at least 100 g (all the plasticine). Use new plates each time. On the Design Sheet, record beside each drawing the weight that bridge would support before collapsing.

5.2 BRIDGE PROBLEM

Name _____

Carefully cut out the river outline and the three plates.

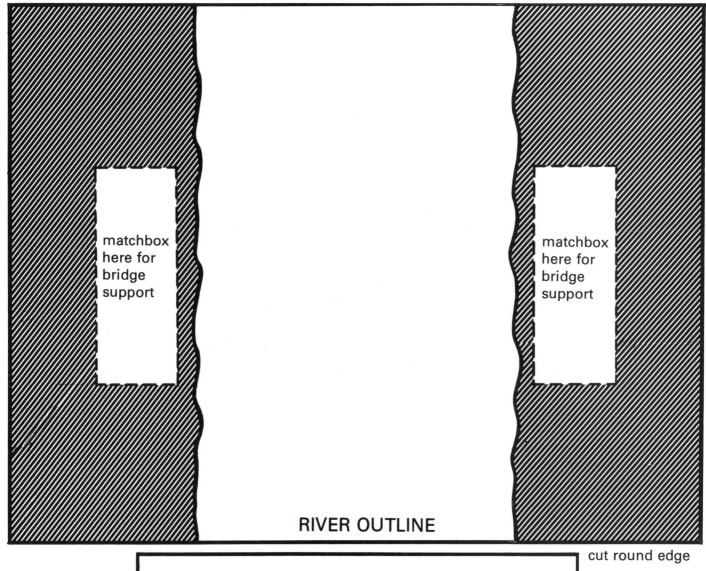

matchbox here for bridge support

matchbox here for bridge support

RIVER OUTLINE

cut round edge

steel plate 1

cut

steel plate 2

cut

steel plate 3

PRINT ON PAPER

5.3   BEAM SHAPES   Design tester _____

1. Cut out the plates from sheet 5.4.

2. You must use each *two* plates to make beams to build a different type of bridge. Start with the ideas on this sheet, using the river crossing from the bridge problem.

3. Don't forget to use two different plates for each new bridge, to give a fair test.

4. Test each design with plasticine weights until it collapses. Note the weight to cause collapse, and record it in the table.

bridge design	basic shape	weight to cause collapse
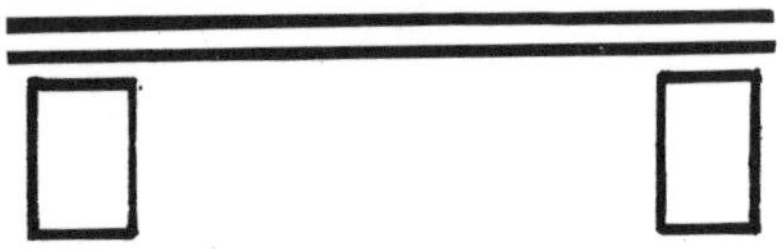	flat plate	
	arch 	
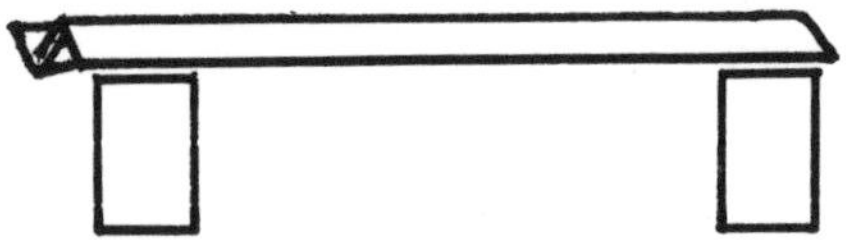	angle girder 	
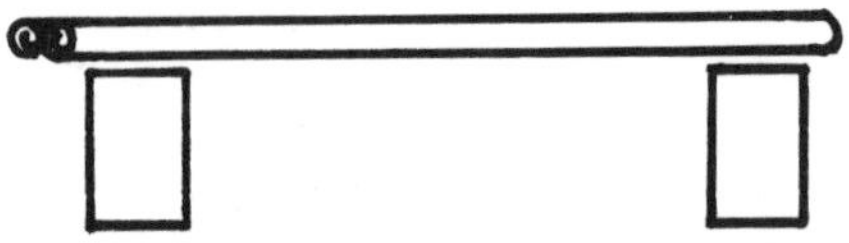	tube 	
? your design	?	

5. Which beam shapes gave the strongest bridges?

_____

_____

5.4 BEAM SHAPES

Name _____

```
cut
cut

cut
```

flat plates

```
cut
cut

cut
```

arches

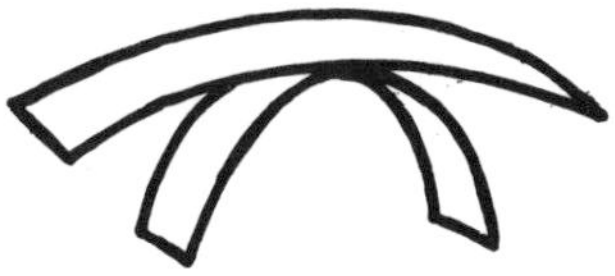

```
cut
- - - - - - - - - fold - - - - - - - - -
cut
- - - - - - - - - fold - - - - - - - - -
cut
```

angle girders

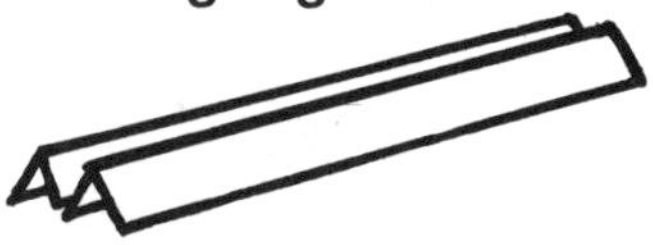

```
cut
cut

cut
```

tubes

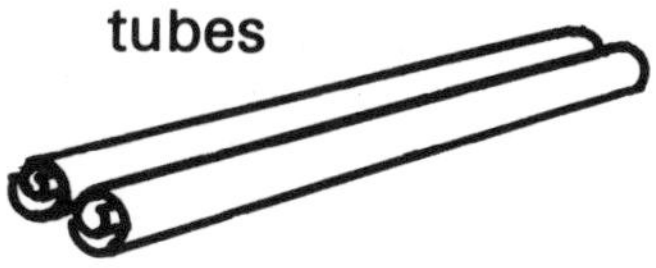

```
cut
cut

cut
```

Your own design?

1. When beams or girders are joined together, they make a type of structure called a 'framework'.

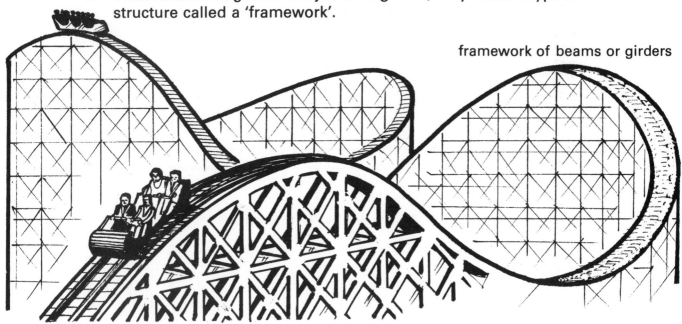

framework of beams or girders

2. The design of these structures is very important. The aim is to build a very strong, rigid framework using as little material as possible.

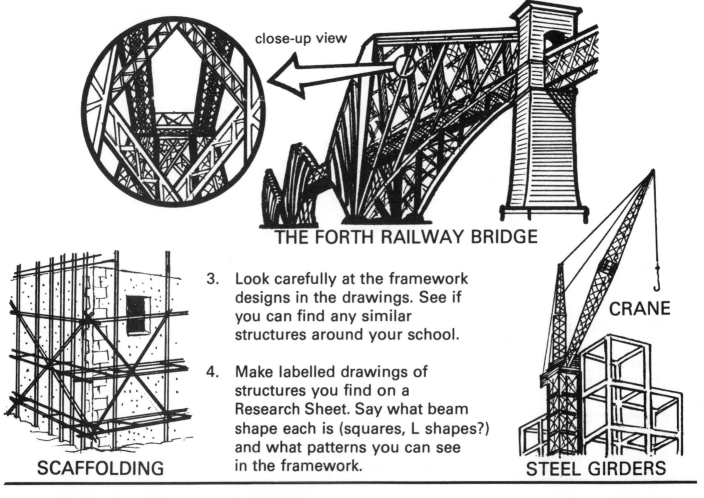

close-up view

THE FORTH RAILWAY BRIDGE

3. Look carefully at the framework designs in the drawings. See if you can find any similar structures around your school.

4. Make labelled drawings of structures you find on a Research Sheet. Say what beam shape each is (squares, L shapes?) and what patterns you can see in the framework.

CRANE

SCAFFOLDING

STEEL GIRDERS

6.2 TOWER PROBLEM

1. A tower is a high structure built by joining many beams or girders. Sometimes you can see the framework, as in the Eiffel Tower. Sometimes the framework is filled in with bricks or concrete walls, as in tower blocks of flats or offices.

2. You have to design a tower with only ten beams. Using ten pipecleaners to represent the beams, build as high a tower as you can. Your finished tower must be able to support 100 g of plasticine.

3. You can cut the beams and bend them into different shapes. You can use extra plasticine to stick the framework to the desk, but no other materials must be used. Twist the ends of the pipecleaners together to join beams.

4. Draw a plan of your tower on a Design Sheet before you build it. Then build and test it with the plasticine. If it collapses, you must design a stronger tower.

5. Beside each design, record the height of the tower, and the weight that caused collapse.

6.3 SIMPLE FRAMEWORKS

Design tester _____

1. You are going to make different frameworks from pipecleaners, in the same way that beams or girders would be used in building, and test the strength of each design.

2. You must use as few pipecleaners as possible for each framework, to keep the cost down. Start with the ideas given on this sheet. Twist the ends tightly together to join the pipecleaners.

3. To test a framework, lay it *flat* on the desk and pull gently on opposite joins, as shown. Repeat, this time pressing the shape. Is it rigid or does it need strengthened? Enter your results in the table.

shape of framework	number of pipecleaners to make rigid	final shape of rigid framework
square		
pentagon		
gate		

4. Which simple shape gave the most rigid framework? _____

5. What did you notice about the strengthening strips? Do they always need to be joined to the corners of a framework? _____

7.1 PROPELLER TESTING

Design tester _____

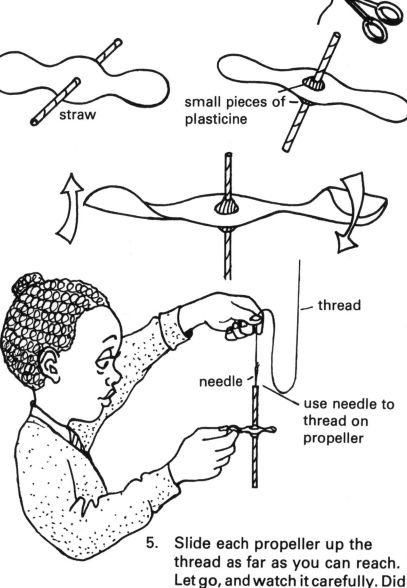

cut out carefully

1. You are going to test the performance of different propeller designs. Carefully cut out one of the propellers from sheet 7.2. Make a small hole in the centre.

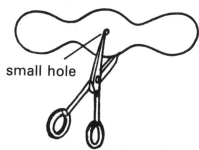

small hole

straw

small pieces of plasticine

2. Push a plastic straw through the hole, and secure it with small pieces of plasticine. Twist the blades as shown.

3. Make a test unit by attaching a strong thread to the ceiling, with a hook or drawing pin. The thread should reach the floor.

thread

needle

use needle to thread on propeller

4. Knot a large darning needle at the end of the thread. Use the needle to thread on each propeller for testing. Stick the needle into a ball of plasticine on the floor, to keep the thread taut.

slide propeller up thread as high as you can reach

let go

does propeller spin well?

plasticine

5. Slide each propeller up the thread as far as you can reach. Let go, and watch it carefully. Did it spin well?

6. Test all the designs on sheet 7.2. Which one spins best?

7. Use a Design Sheet to draw propeller shapes of your own. Cut out each design in thin card and test it. Try different amounts of twist in the blades to see if that improves their performance. Keep a note of the test results beside each design.

Name _____

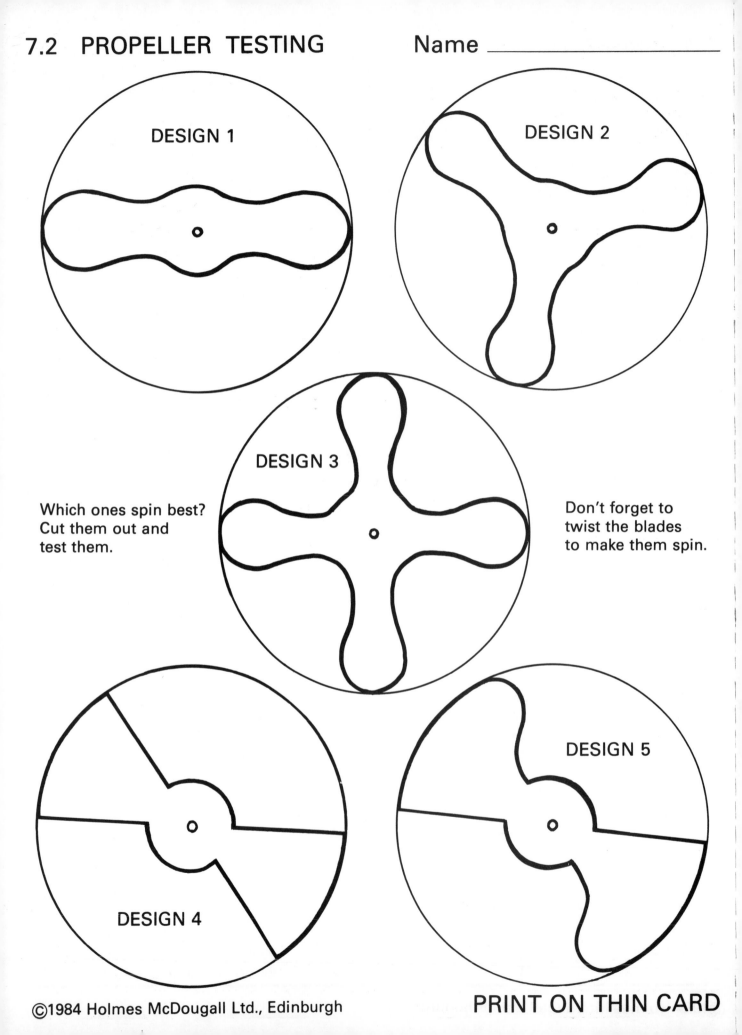

DESIGN 1

DESIGN 2

DESIGN 3

Which ones spin best?
Cut them out and
test them.

Don't forget to
twist the blades
to make them spin.

DESIGN 4

DESIGN 5

PRINT ON THIN CARD

7.3 POWER BOAT

Name _____

1. You are going to make a working model of a propeller-driven boat.

2. Cut a plastic bottle as shown and put plasticine in the bottom.

3. Cut a piece of card to fit the space in the bottle. Cut out and colour the outline of a ship. Fix this into the plasticine.

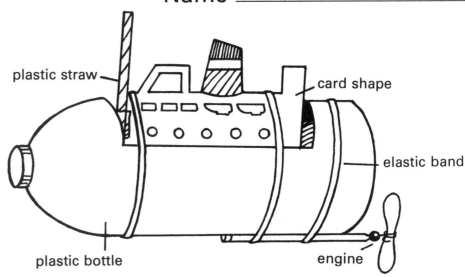

plastic straw

card shape

elastic band

plastic bottle

engine

MAKING THE ENGINE

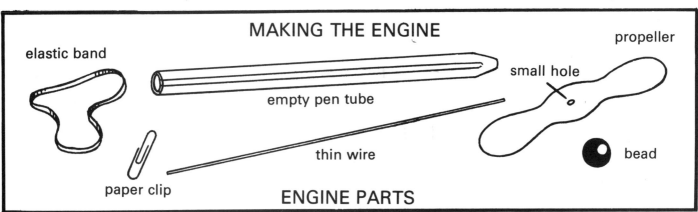

elastic band

empty pen tube

propeller

small hole

thin wire

paper clip

bead

ENGINE PARTS

---

4. Bend a small hook in thin wire. Fix on an elastic band. Attach a paper clip to the free end of the elastic.

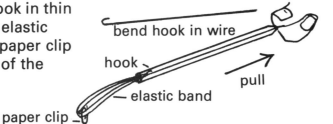

bend hook in wire

hook

elastic band

pull

paper clip

5. Pull the wire and elastic through a pen tube as shown. Open out the clip and tape it to the end of the tube.

6. Fit a bead and then a propeller to the wire. The wire goes through a hole in the centre of the propeller and is then wrapped round it. Twist the propeller blades to shape them.

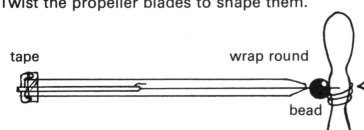

tape

wrap round

bead

twist

twist

7. Fix the engine below your boat. Wind it up and test it.

8. Time the boat over a given distance and work out its speed. Have a competition with your friends for the fastest power-boat.

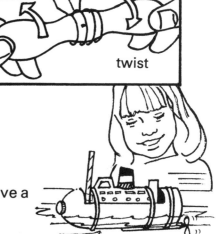

Scientific Problem Solving
LEVEL 2

Teacher's notes on the eight topics

1 Test flight

1.1 and 1.2	X wing starship
1.3	Test flight game

2 Parachutes

2.1	Parachutes
2.2	Parachute release problem
2.3 and 2.4	Parachute release devices
2.5	Parachute release lever

3 Electricity

3.1	Electrical conductors
3.2	Stage lighting problem
3.3	Ideas for dimmers

4 Sensing devices

4.1	Water level indicator
4.2	Ideas for switches

5 Pawl and ratchet

5.1 and 5.2	Pawl and ratchet
5.3	Ideas for using pawl and ratchet

6 Keys and alarms

6.1	Which key?
6.2	Make a key card
6.3	Which key card?
6.4	Beat the burglar!
6.5	Ideas for keys and alarms

7 Archimedes' screw

7.1	Wire bridge problem
7.2	Wire bridge problem solved
7.3 and 7.4	Marble dispensers

8 Mechanical arms

8.1, 8.2, and 8.3	Mechanical arms
8.4	An extending arm
8.5	Danger—radioactive!
8.6	An extractor

TEACHER'S NOTES

1 Test flight

Aims
a To develop awareness of how a model (an X wing starship) can be used to gauge the performance of real prototypes.
b To give experience in the devising, construction and testing of a launch device for use with the model.
c To compete in a simple 'points' game involving the accurate use of the launcher and starship.

Procedure
a Issue X WING STARSHIP (1.1 and 1.2) to all pupils, with the necessary materials. 1.1 introduces the idea of how engineers and scientists test and modify accurate models before building costly full-size prototypes. This gives a sound reason for making and testing the futuristic starship model. The problem is to devise a method of launching the model. A clue is given that the device should be capable of launching the X wing at different speeds and inclinations, suggesting the need to calibrate the launcher in some way. Plans should be worked out on a Design Sheet first.
b Sheet 1.2 gives details of construction and cutouts for making the model. The wings can be taped or glued to the top part of the body section. A weight is needed in the nose and a marble-sized piece of plasticine can be used inside the body. A paper clip taped to the nose at an angle adds weight and acts as a neat grip for an elastic band launcher.
c TEST FLIGHT GAME (1.3) can be used at your discretion. The sheet also gives a possible method of making a launcher. Issue this part of the sheet only to those in difficulty, or unsure of how to calibrate their device. In this design, the greater the stretch of the elastic, the faster the launch speed and thus the distance travelled *for a set angle.* The angle of launch can be adjusted by moving the brick.

Notes
a Some background science work may be necessary on the principles of flight (birds, balloons, planes, rockets, etc.).
b It is worth stressing to pupils that models used in applied science and engineering are much more precise replicas of full scale machines, and work to finer tolerances than is possible using paper or card.
c Pupils may devise other methods for projecting the X wing, which should be encouraged, e.g. firing from a plastic bottle, as shown.

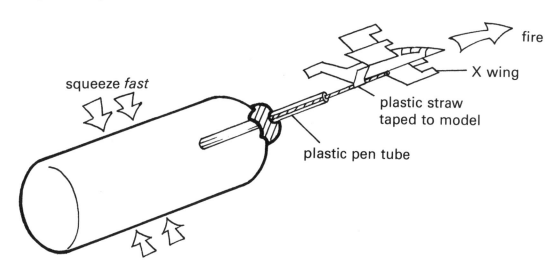

squeeze *fast*

fire

X wing

plastic straw taped to model

plastic pen tube

This method is often very successful, although it is difficult to control the force at launch and this makes the flight unpredictable. The angle of take off can be estimated, however.

Follow-up work

Issue Research Sheets and ask pupils to devise their own model aeroplanes using, perhaps, the same body pattern but changing the number and/or shape of the wings. Ask them to explain their reasons for thinking one design better than another.

Materials

(for each pupil)	(for groups)
Sheets 1.1 and 1.2	brick or wood block
Sheet 1.3 as required	cardboard (boxes, sheets, tubes)
Design Sheet	drawing pins
colours	elastic bands
glue	metre stick
paper clips	nails and small hammer
plasticine/putty	paper clips
scissors	plastic bags and bottles
sticky tape	plastic pen tubes
	plastic straws
	plasticine/putty
	protractor
	springs
	sticky tape
	strong thread/thin string
	wire (iron, garden type)
	wire snips
	wood pieces

In addition to these basic materials, children should have access to a variety of everyday items from hardware and toy shop, to allow for alternative solutions to those shown.

2   Parachutes

Aims

a   To construct and test a simple model parachute.

b   To develop problem-solving skills through creative design, practical ingenuity and experimental testing of a device for releasing the parachute from a height.

Procedure

a   PARACHUTES (2.1) should be issued to all pupils. The instructions describe a simple way of making a model parachute from a square of thin polythene, after practising on newspaper. The parachute is tested by hand release prior to the main problem, of release from a height, being posed.

b   PARACHUTE RELEASE PROBLEM (2.2) can then be issued. Pupils have to devise a mechanism which will enable a parachute to be released from a height of three metres. The illustration deliberately gives no clue to the design of the release mechanism, other than showing that the parachute hangs from a projection (so that it falls clear of the pole). Encourage them to think of ideas, plan on a Design Sheet, and get your approval before making up their first prototype.

c   The Test Report will involve pupils in timing and taking average results from, say, three tries. Accuracy is not possible with the crude mechanisms used, more important is whether or not the devices will operate when the parachute weight is increased. Many simple mechanisms fail to work at this stage. Ask pupils to improve the construction or think of a new design.

d PARACHUTE RELEASE DEVICES (2.3 and 2.4) give a variety of solutions to the problem, some better than others. All require to be constructed efficiently in order to work. Use these sheets as you think necessary, cut up and given to those who are totally without ideas; have met problems and need a clue to enable them to *modify their own device* and achieve success; or have had success with one mechanism and can profitably be asked to compare theirs with a different device.

e PARACHUTE RELEASE LEVER (2.5) has instructions for making a cardboard device for releasing the parachute. This solution could be used for group or class, or given to those who fail to come up with anything. The elastic band must be thin and not too tight, or it can be omitted and the device still works well with light loads.

Notes

a Background science work may be necessary on air and air resistance so that pupils appreciate how a parachute works.

b Making the parachute sometimes gives problems, which can waste a lot of polythene, therefore newspaper is suggested for initial trials. Make sure they cut the correct corner!

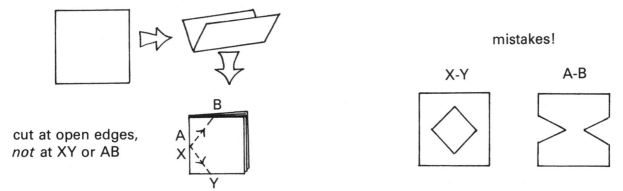

mistakes!

cut at open edges,
not at XY or AB

X-Y   A-B

c Testing of the parachutes can be done at desk height to start with, from the end of a ruler or metre stick. *Successful* release devices can then be fitted to a long pole.

d If the electromagnet release device is used, pupils should be told that the battery will run down very quickly if it is kept on for long periods of time. This method does not work well with heavy loads.

e The pneumatic and hydraulic release devices can be used with great success. (See Starting Technology 1, Robots.)

Follow-up work

Issue Research Sheets and ask pupils to list, with simple labelled diagrams, the uses of parachutes.

Materials

(for each pupil)

Sheets 2.1 and 2.2
Sheets 2.3, 2.4 and 2.5 as required
metre stick or similar
plasticine/putty
scissors
square of thin polythene (bin liner)
squares of newspaper
sticky tape
strong thread/thin string

(for groups)

balance for weights
4½ V battery
bell wire (plastic-covered copper wire)
card pieces
clothes pegs
drawing pins
elastic bands
eyelet screws/small cuphooks
glue
hairpins
lolly sticks

long pole (3 metres)
nails and small hammer
paper fasteners
pencils
plastic bags, bottles, straws, tubs
plastic syringes, plastic tubing
plasticine/putty
pliers
springs
sticky tape
strong thread/thin string
wire and wire snips
wood pieces

In addition to these basic materials, children should have access to a variety of everyday items from hardware and toy shop, to allow for alternative solutions to those shown.

3   Electricity

Aims
a   To extend understanding of electrical conductors through systematic testing and recording of experimental observations.
b   To apply the results of the experiments to designing a practical dimmer device for use in a model.

Procedure
a   ELECTRICAL CONDUCTORS (3.1) uses a series circuit for testing a variety of materials, and should be issued with the necessary materials to all pupils. The results table has been designed so that they will grasp that some materials conduct electricity better than others, and that the distance apart of the connections makes a difference. Aluminium foil is a good conductor and the length of the foil makes little difference to the brightness of the bulb. A long iron wire or carbon (pencil lead) causes the bulb to dim considerably compared with a short piece of the same material. In a similar way, the further apart the wires are in the salty water, the more the bulb will dim.

b   Before issuing the next sheet, it is hoped that most children will have concluded that it is possible to use these materials to make a device which will gradually dim a bulb (see *f* below).

c   Issue STAGE LIGHTING PROBLEM (3.2) and discuss what lighting effects are required in a theatre. Some children may have experience of the real thing, and can explain why dimming the lights is necessary. It is probably easier to make up the model theatre beforehand as shown, and supply a selection of materials for making a dimmer. Pupils then only have to join up the bulbs and connect them to a battery and their dimmer devices. The wires should be long enough so that wiring up can take place on a desk top.

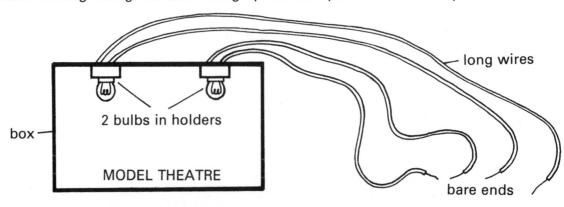

box —

2 bulbs in holders

MODEL THEATRE

long wires

bare ends

d   Ideas for the design of a dimmer should be worked out on Design Sheets and seen by you before construction begins. Allow pupils considerable freedom at this stage, but consider carefully the practical difficulties inherent in their proposals.

e   IDEAS FOR DIMMERS (3.3) is intended for those in difficulty, or wishing to compare their dimmer with another design or a different method. Use the parts of the sheet as required.

f   Pupils may come up with a solution where one bulb goes out while the other remains lit. This partly solves the problem, but make it clear that this is an unsatisfactory solution because the light is not dim enough, and the theatre is not uniformly lit.

Acceptable solutions are:

Wire   A successful dimmer is made by winding wire tightly around a piece of thick card or smooth wood. The main difficulty, which pupils should be encouraged to overcome, is in achieving good electrical contact with the sliding arm. Using foil with an elastic band to give contact pressure will help.

Carbon (pencil lead)   Keeping good electrical contact while sliding the wire along the lead can be solved as above.

Salty water   Results are not so predictable because the wire separation is difficult to adjust and maintain. The method is clearly not so convenient as the others.

With the two terminals A and B at different distances apart in the salty water, the bulbs can be made to dim and brighten.

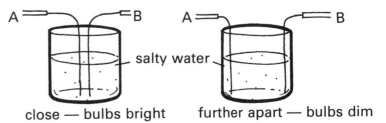

close — bulbs bright   further apart — bulbs dim

Notes

a   Background science work is necessary to ensure that pupils understand the simple electrical circuit, conductors and insulators.

b   It may be useful to have pupils explore ways of wiring two bulbs (series and parallel connections) prior to posing the problem sheet. The bulbs are best wired in parallel so that if one fails then the circuit remains lit, as shown:

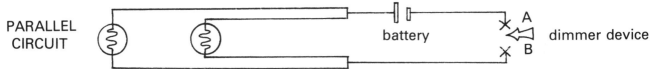

PARALLEL CIRCUIT   battery   dimmer device

c   Warn children NEVER to try experiments with mains electricity — it can kill.

Follow-up work

Issue Research Sheets and ask pupils to find out about house lighting (switches, circuits, meter, etc.) and how electricity is supplied to their homes from power stations.

Materials (for each pupil)

ELECTRICAL CONDUCTORS
Sheet 3.1
aluminium foil
3 V or 4½ V battery
bell wire (plastic-covered copper wire)
bulb in holder
copper coin
long lead pencils
thin iron, nichrome or manganin wire
water

plastic tub
plasticine/putty
salt
scissors
screwdriver
spoon

STAGE LIGHTING PROBLEM
Sheet 3.2
Sheet 3.3 as required
Design Sheet
items as for ELECTRICAL CONDUCTORS,
    plus model theatre
card pieces
paper fasteners
sticky tape

In addition to these basic materials, children should have access to a variety of everyday items from hardware and toy shop, to allow for alternative solutions to those shown.

4 Sensing devices

Aims
a To give experience of the design, testing and development of one application of a simple electrical switch.
b To develop an awareness of automatic control in operation.

Procedure
a WATER LEVEL INDICATOR (4.1) should be issued to all pupils with a selection of materials and the problem discussed. They have to devise a mechanism which will switch on a bulb when the water level is about 5 cm from the top of a container. Such a warning device is recognised by children as being very useful.
b Any solutions suggested can be planned on a Design Sheet and examined for practicality before you allow construction to go ahead. Aim for simple mechanisms which are not over-demanding in their requirements, but allow ingenious solutions to be tried out.
c IDEAS FOR SWITCHES (4.2) outlines in labelled diagrams four possible devices which will operate the bulb. Cut this sheet up and use it as required, for example to assist those in difficulties or without ideas; to help improve a similar design; to assist pupils to make good drawings of their own device; to highlight the advantages of clear labelled diagrams as opposed to long verbal descriptions of complex mechanisms. Try asking them to describe in words how to make any of the devices on Sheet 4.2!

Notes
Background science work is essential before attempting this topic, to ensure that pupils understand the simple electrical circuit, conductors and insulators.

Follow-up work
a Individuals or small 'Research and Development' groups can be asked to design and make a device which puts a sensor to good use. For example, a warning light when the water level falls to a very low mark — well understood from petrol gauges, etc. The previous solution may be used with adaptations, but encourage pupils to come up with their own ideas. The problem is best tackled with a large size container which allows things to be fixed inside.
b Issue Research Sheets and ask pupils to use books and magazines to list instances, with diagrams where possible, when warning lights are used (e.g. traffic lights, alarms, flashing beacons). Mention purpose, colours, timing, etc.

Materials (for groups)

Sheet 4.1 for each pupil
Sheet 4.2 as required
Design Sheet for each pupil
aluminium foil
3 V or 4½ V battery
bell wire (plastic-covered copper wire)
bulb in holder
card pieces
corks (various sizes)
drawing pins
elastic bands
glue
large plastic drinks bottle/ice cream tub

lolly sticks
nails (various sizes) and hammer
paper clips, fasteners, hairpins, pins, etc.
plastic bags, cups, pen tubes, straws
plastic tubing
plasticine/putty
polystyrene pieces
rubbers
ruler
scissors
screwdriver
sticky tape
strong thread/thin string
wood (small pieces and blocks)

In addition to these basic materials, children should have access to a variety of everyday items from hardware and toy shop, to allow for alternative solutions to those shown.

5 Pawl and ratchet

Aims

a To introduce and establish the principle of the pawl and ratchet.

b To given practice in the construction, testing and modification of such a mechanism.

c To promote ingenuity in the practical application of the pawl and ratchet.

Procedure

a Ideally, the pawl and ratchet mechanism could first be 'discovered' and studied in an object such as a fishing reel, bicycle, or old clock. It can, however, be introduced satisfactorily by simply issuing PAWL AND RATCHET (5.1 and 5.2) and guiding pupils in the construction of the card model. It is important to cut out the ratchet wheels as carefully as possible and glue them together in alignment to make one thick wheel.

b You can ask individuals or small 'Research and Development' groups to use a Design Sheet to design and then build something to show how the pawl and ratchet can be put to good use.

c IDEAS FOR USING PAWL AND RATCHET (5.3) is available if you find it necessary to assist pupils in difficulty or without ideas; to help improve a similar design; or for those who have had success with one mechanism and can profitably be asked to compare theirs with a different device.

Notes

Background science work could be useful before attempting this topic, so that pupils understand the principles of gear wheels, but this is not essential.

Follow-up work

a Issue Research Sheets and ask pupils to use books or magazines to list or draw machines which use a pawl and ratchet. Remind them that although the device may look different, it is still the same mechanism.

b Consider possible applications of the pawl and ratchet in other areas covered by this book, e.g. marble dispensers (7.3 and 7.4).

c The finished models, painted and trimmed, can be displayed in an end of term Technology Exhibition.

Materials

PAWL AND RATCHET (for each pupil)
Sheets 5.1 and 5.2
drawing pins
elastic bands
glue
paper clips
scissors
sticky tape
wooden board or cork tile

IDEAS FOR USING PAWL AND RATCHET (individuals or groups)
Sheet 5.3 as required
Design Sheet
cardboard (thick and thin)
cotton reels
craft knife
drawing pins
knitting needles
metal brackets (L-shaped)
nails and small hammer
paper clips, fasteners, hairpins, pins, etc.
plastic bottles and containers
plastic straws
plasticine/putty
scissors
screws and screwdriver
sticky tape
strong thread/thin string
wire (iron, garden type)
wire snips
wood pieces/cork tiles

In addition to these basic materials, children should have access to a variety of everyday items from hardware and toy shop, to allow for alternative solutions to those shown.

6 Keys and alarms

Aims
a To consolidate understanding and give practice in setting up simple electrical circuits.
b To foster accuracy and observation, manual precision and inventiveness.

Procedure
a Sheets one to five need not be regarded as a sequence, but you may find it valuable to do 6.2 and 6.3 first. 6.1 is optional.
b WHICH KEY? (6.1) is essentially an exercise in close scrutiny and the important feature is for pupils to check to make sure that their answer is correct. Use it as a starter if you need it.
c Issue MAKE A KEY CARD (6.2) and the necessary materials and ask pupils to follow the instructions. You will need to make up the lock and wire it as in the diagram, for them to check their keycards against. Make sure that all electrical connections are clean, dry and firm.
d WHICH KEY CARD? (6.3) is a similar exercise, only more difficult. Again, you will need to make up the lock *exactly* as shown in the diagram. When pupils are testing their cards on your lock, check that each card is pressed accurately and firmly in place.
e BEAT THE BURGLAR! (6.4) is a popular exercise in ingenuity. On issuing the sheet and materials it is probably necessary to discuss the problem. Ask pupils to plan their alarm devices on a Design Sheet before starting to construct them. The cardboard boxes should be large enough to give scope for trying out different devices (at least 30 cm each side).
f IDEAS FOR KEYS AND ALARMS (6.5) can be issued at your discretion. Sometimes it is better to wait until pupils have produced their own ideas. The sheet will help those who have none; or who would benefit from seeing clear labelled diagrams of similar devices, to help them draw their own.

Notes
If you cannot obtain different coloured bulbs for 6.3, simply label the lights on your lock board as in the diagram.

Follow-up work
a Revision or extension work on simple circuits, magnets and electromagnets may trigger off ideas for new alarm patterns. It could be worth while returning to problem 6.4 to allow more inventive or sophisticated solutions to be put into operation.
b This is an excellent type of work for an end of term Technology Exhibition or a competition, which means that the work will remain open for development for some weeks.

Materials

KEYCARDS (for each pupil)	(for yourself)
Sheet 6.1 as required	aluminium foil
Sheets 6.2 and 6.3	four or five 4½ V batteries
aluminium foil	bell wire (plastic-covered copper wire)
card pieces	6 bulbs (white, blue, red, green)
glue	6 bulb holders
pencil	card pieces
scissors	screwdriver
tracing paper	wire snips

BEAT THE BURGLAR! (for individuals or groups)
Sheet 6.4
Sheet 6.5 as required
Design Sheet
aluminium foil
3 V or 4½ V battery
bell wire (plastic-covered copper wire)
bulb with holder
cardboard pieces and boxes
corks (various sizes)
drawing pins
marbles (in bag)
nails and small hammer
paper clips, fasteners, hairpins, pins, etc.
plastic straws
plasticine/putty
scissors
screwdriver
sticky tape
strong thread/thin string
wire snips

In addition to these basic materials, children should have access to a variety of everyday items from hardware and toy shop, to allow for alternative solutions to those shown.

7 Archimedes screw

Aims
a To introduce and establish the principle of the Archimedes screw.
b To use this device to initiate feasibility studies of designs for a marble dispenser and to cultivate an inventive approach to the production of such a mechanism.

Procedure
a Issue WIRE BRIDGE PROBLEM (7.1) with the necessary materials. Act as a referee, if necessary, to ensure that the rules are obeyed. The commonest questions are about the wire — yes, they can take it out, shape it, and put it back in the box again.
b WIRE BRIDGE PROBLEM SOLVED (7.2) should be issued when you judge it to be necessary. Ensure that everyone eventually gets a good working solution, as in diagram 4.
c MARBLE DISPENSERS (7.3 and 7.4) are available to permit an application of the screw technique, and the invention of other devices to produce a working model. Issue Design Sheets for pupils to work out their own ideas.

Follow-up work
a Pupils can be given Research Sheets and asked to investigate dispensers for other objects, e.g. matchboxes, sweets, bars of chocolate, drinks. Find as many machines in use locally as you can.
b The work on Valves (Starting Technology 1) and Pawl and Ratchet (5.1 to 5.3), would be worth referring to, for more ideas of possible practical applications of the Archimedes screw.

Materials

WIRE BRIDGE PROBLEM (for each pupil)
Sheets 7.1 and 7.2
Design Sheet
cardboard box (small/halved)
paper clips

pencils
plasticine/putty
wire (iron, garden type)
wire snips

MARBLE DISPENSERS (for individuals or groups)
Sheets 7.3 and 7.4 as required
Design Sheet
cardboard (boxes, pieces, tubes)
cotton reels
drawing pins, large pins
glue
marbles
nails and small hammer

plastic bottles
plastic straws
scissors
sticky tape
strong thread/thin string
wire (iron, garden type)
wire snips
wood blocks (small)

In addition to these basic materials, children should have access to a variety of everyday items from hardware and toy shop, to allow for alternative solutions to those shown.

8   Mechanical arms

Aims

a   To provide a number of ideas for the construction and use of mechanical handling devices.

b   To foster inventive design, development, modification and testing of these devices.

Procedure

a   Issue MECHANICAL ARMS (8.1 and 8.2) first, with the necessary materials, and guide pupils in the construction of a good working model. When this is satisfactorily completed, a model with more than two fingers should be attempted. They can work out ideas on a Design Sheet before extending the model arm.

b   MECHANICAL ARMS (8.3), which contains a possible solution to the problem of adding extra fingers to the arm, plus further developments in 'bioengineering', should be issued at your discretion. Suggest that either item 2 *or* 3 is attempted by individual children.

c   Cut off the 'Emergency Notice' from the foot of 8.4 (AN EXTENDING ARM) for later use, then issue the rest of the sheet. Guide pupils in the construction of this arm, checking that the pieces are assembled in the correct manner. It is very important to fix the joints together accurately, in the positions marked.

d   Then issue DANGER — RADIOACTIVE! (8.5) and allow pupils to follow the instructions and practise moving a drawing pin between the two 'reaction chambers'. When all are expert at this, simulate an emergency by handing round the 'Emergency Notice', and pressure them into producing a speedy solution to the problem.

e   AN EXTRACTOR (8.6) should be issued along with the necessary materials and guidance given in the construction of this kind of handling device. Pupils should then use a Design Sheet to plan an improved or longer version.

Notes

a   The best materials for handling with the mechanical arm are soft fabrics or foam pieces.

b   A plastic drinks bottle can be prepared as shown so that pupils can extract objects from it:

small hole for extractor
to enter bottle

soft items (e.g. foam pieces)
small enough to be pulled out
through hole

Some teachers have elaborated on this idea — the bottle has been dressed as a patient, and the extractor has become a surgical instrument. Others have developed the 'ship in a bottle' approach with very attractive results. However you develop this sort of activity, try to create further problems so that variants of the extracting tool become necessary and are designed and built by the children.

Follow-up work
Further investigation of specialised handling tools and notes on their design and use should be recorded on Research Sheets as the opportunity presents itself.

Materials (for each pupil)

MECHANICAL ARMS
Sheets 8.1 and 8.2
Sheet 8.3 as required
Design Sheet
card pieces
colours
drawing pins
glue
paper fasteners
plastic straws
scissors
sticky tape
strong thread/thin string

AN EXTENDING ARM
Sheets 8.4 and 8.5
card pieces
colours
drawing pins
paper clips, fasteners
scissors
sticky tape

AN EXTRACTOR
Sheet 8.6
Design Sheet as required
foam (small pieces)
plastic bottle (large)
plastic straws
scissors
sticky tape
wire (iron, garden type)
wire snips

In addition to these basic materials, children should have access to a variety of everyday items from hardware and toy shop, to allow for alternative solutions to those shown.

1.1 X WING STARSHIP

Aeronautics engineer _____

X WING STARSHIP
ON A JOURNEY
BETWEEN SPACE STATIONS

1. Before building a new type of machine, scientists and engineers usually make models and test them. Design improvements can then be made if needed.

2. Look at the plans on sheet 1.2 for the model of this X wing starship. Read the instructions carefully, then make the model.

3. Before you can test the performance of your starship, you will need to design a launcher. This should be placed on the floor, and designed so that you can launch the starship
   a at different speeds,
   b at different angles of ascent.

LAUNCHER

speed (fast or slow)
starship flight

gentle ascent

speed (fast or slow)
starship flight

steep ascent

4. Your teacher will give you the materials to help you build a launcher. Work out your plans on a Design Sheet first, and list the things you will need. After testing, record beside the design how well your launcher worked.

1.2 X WING STARSHIP

Name ______________________

1. Cut out the body and wings of the starship. Fold and tape the body as shown.

2. Bend the wings to slot into the body. Colour the finished model.

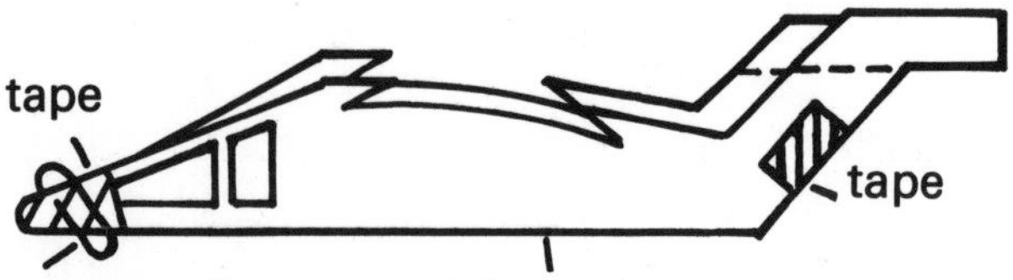

tape
tape
paper clip set at an angle
fold body

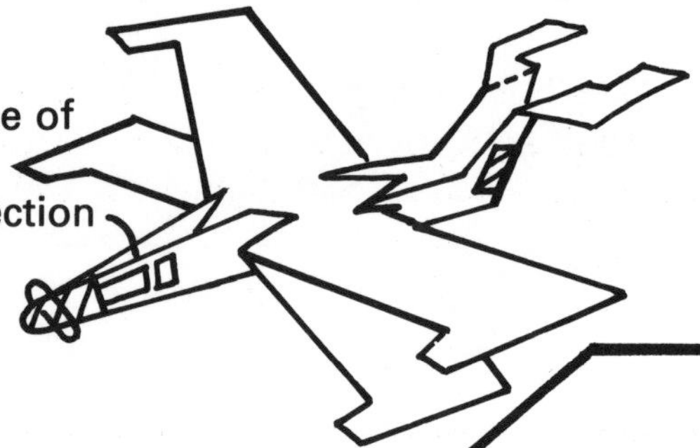

small piece of plasticine in nose section

STARSHIP BODY

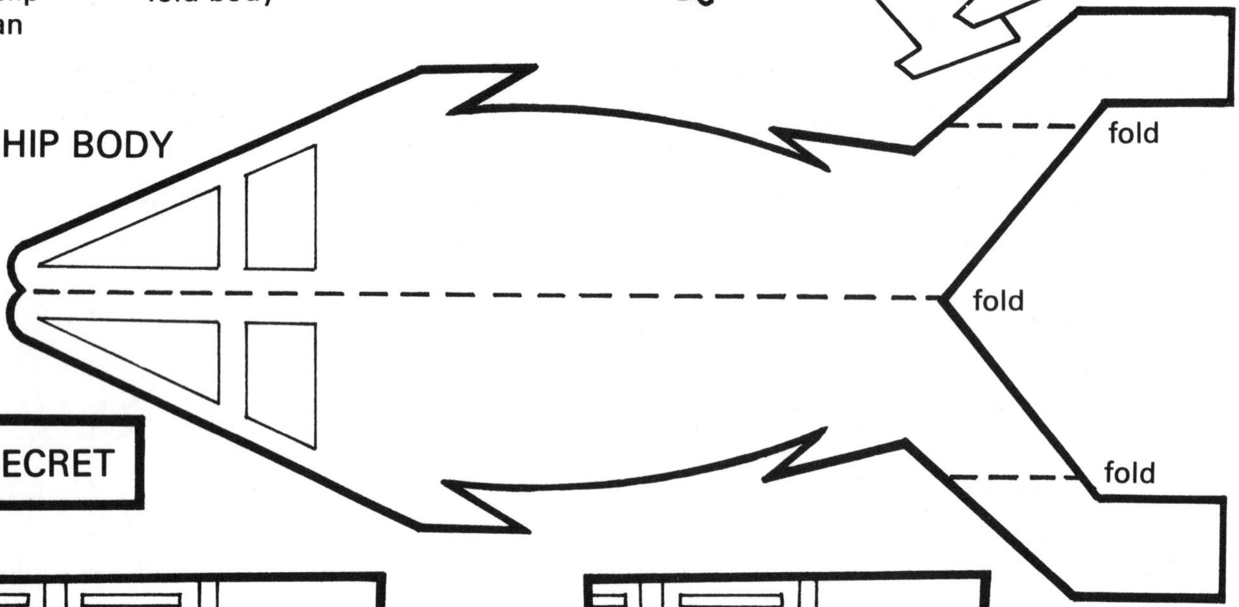

fold
fold
fold
fold

TOP SECRET

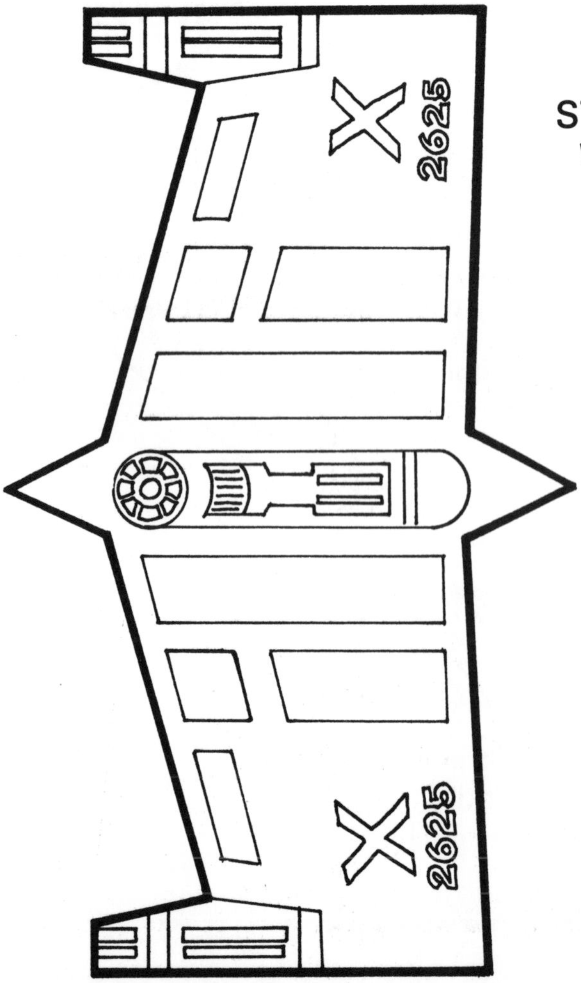

X 2625
X 2625

STARSHIP WINGS

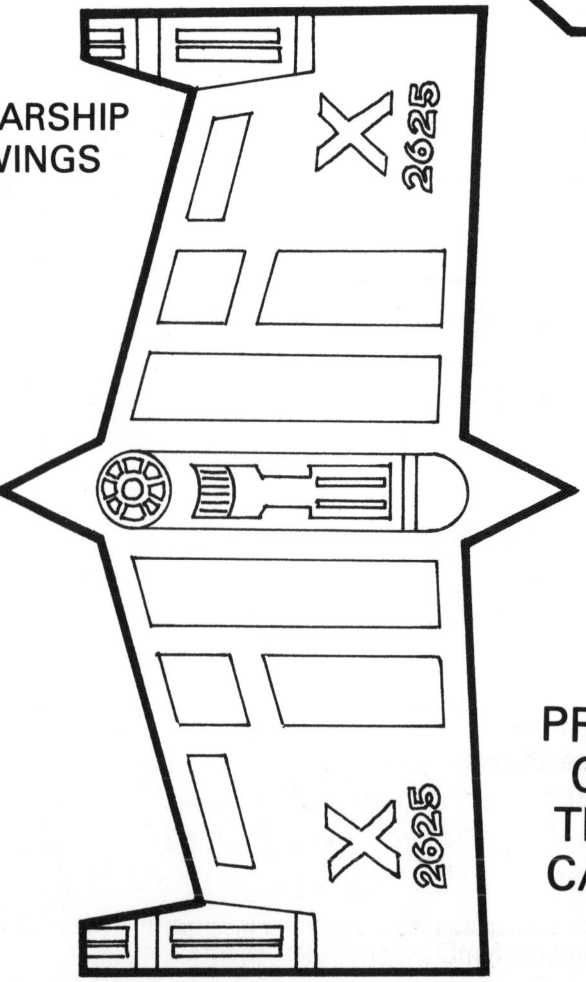

X 2625
X 2625

PRINT ON THIN CARD

1.3 TEST FLIGHT GAME

Test pilot _____

1. Test the X wing starship using your launcher. Play a 'points' game with a friend. Fly your starship and try to make it land at an agreed distance from launch.

2. Use the following flight table to start with. Chalk circles on the floor as shown to make a target.

FLIGHT SCORE SHEET	HIT = 3 NEAR = 1 MISS = 0	
	you	friend
1 ✕ launch ————— 3 m ————→ ③ 1 (30 cm / 60 cm)		
2 ✕ launch ————— 4 m ————→ ③ 1		
3 ✕ launch — 1 m — [chair or desk] ✕ — 3 m — ③ 1		
4 ✕ launch ——→ farthest in *one* shot wins (*over* 4 m = 3 points, *under* 4 m = 1 point)		
	TOTAL		

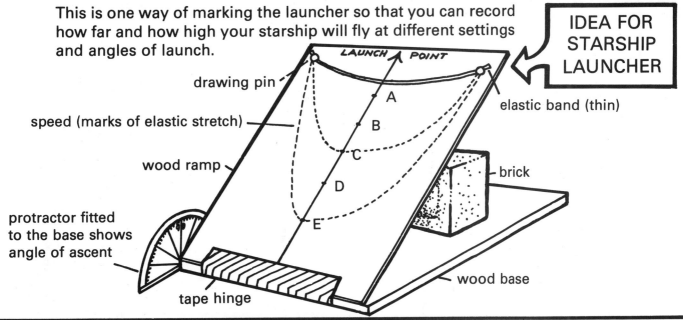

This is one way of marking the launcher so that you can record how far and how high your starship will fly at different settings and angles of launch.

IDEA FOR STARSHIP LAUNCHER

LAUNCH POINT

drawing pin

A
B
C
D
E

elastic band (thin)

speed (marks of elastic stretch)

wood ramp

brick

protractor fitted to the base shows angle of ascent

tape hinge

wood base

1. You are going to carry out tests on a working model parachute.

2. Make a parachute following the design below. Use newspaper for your first trials. When you are happy with the design, cut the same shape from thin polythene.

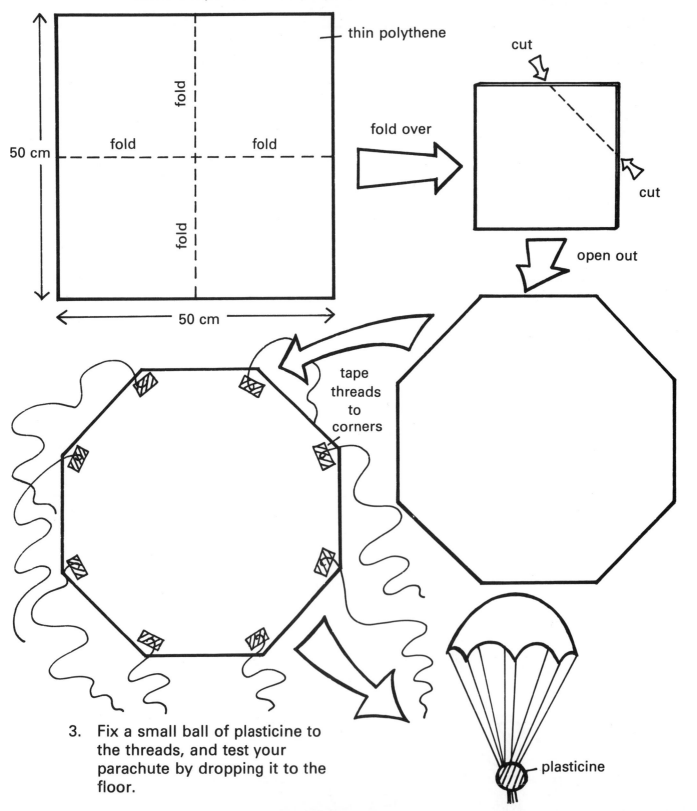

thin polythene

fold

fold

fold

fold

50 cm

50 cm

fold over

cut

cut

open out

tape threads to corners

plasticine

3. Fix a small ball of plasticine to the threads, and test your parachute by dropping it to the floor.

2.2 PARACHUTE RELEASE PROBLEM

Designer _____

1. The parachute has now to be released from a height of about three metres. You have to measure the time it takes to reach the floor.

2. The problem you must solve is to make a simple device which will allow you to release the parachute from this height, at the end of a long pole.

3. Your teacher will give you the materials to make a release mechanism. Draw or write down your ideas on a Design Sheet, listing the things you will need, before you start to build it.

4. TEST REPORT
   Test your release mechanism with different weights of plasticine.

   Keep a table of results for the time (in seconds) your parachute took to fall with 10 g, 50 g, 100 g, and 200 g weights on the end.

   You could take the average time from three tries for each weight, to make the test fairer.

release device

parachute

3 m pole

2.3 PARACHUTE RELEASE DEVICES

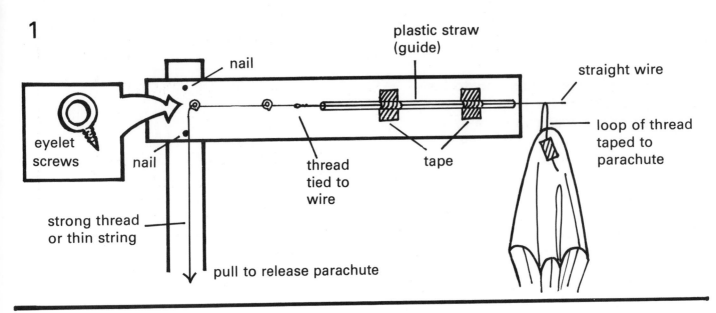

1

eyelet screws

nail

nail

plastic straw (guide)

straight wire

thread tied to wire

tape

loop of thread taped to parachute

strong thread or thin string

pull to release parachute

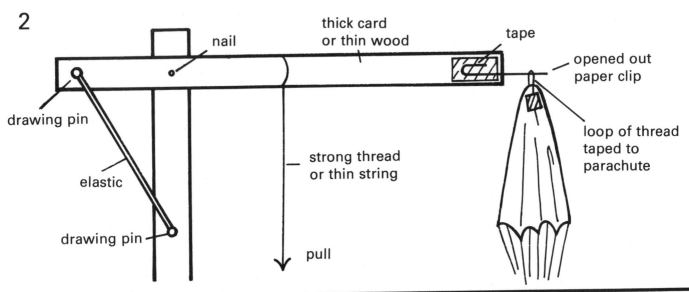

2

nail

thick card or thin wood

tape

opened out paper clip

drawing pin

elastic

drawing pin

strong thread or thin string

loop of thread taped to parachute

pull

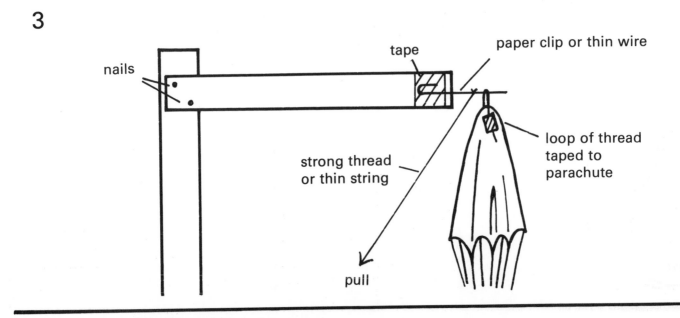

3

nails

tape

paper clip or thin wire

strong thread or thin string

loop of thread taped to parachute

pull

2.4 PARACHUTE RELEASE DEVICES

4 ELECTROMAGNET

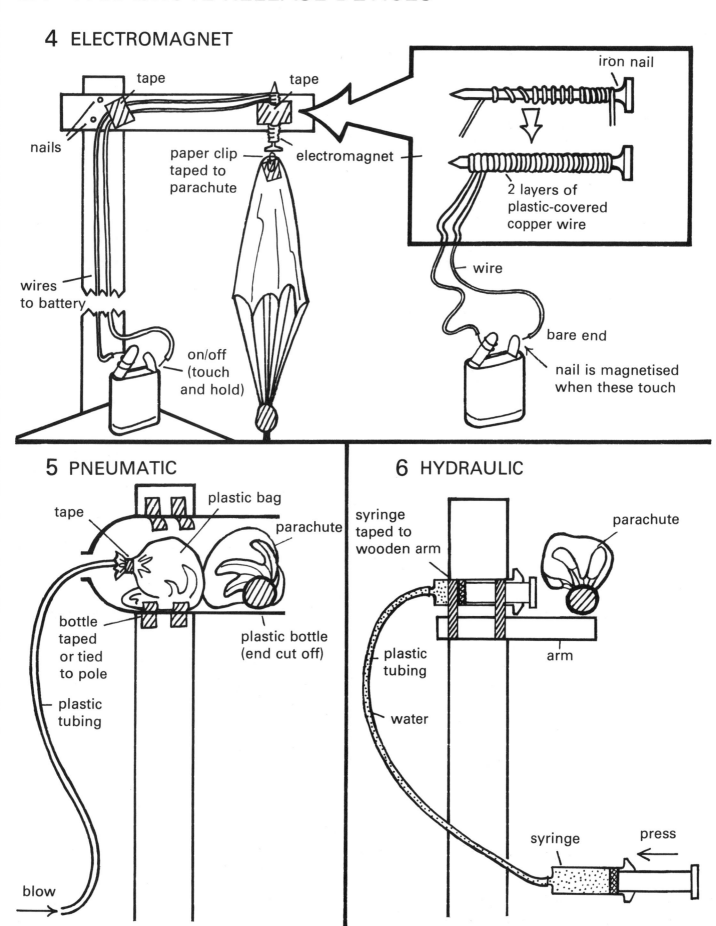

tape

tape

nails

paper clip taped to parachute

electromagnet

wires to battery

on/off (touch and hold)

iron nail

2 layers of plastic-covered copper wire

wire

bare end

nail is magnetised when these touch

5 PNEUMATIC

tape

plastic bag

parachute

bottle taped or tied to pole

plastic tubing

plastic bottle (end cut off)

blow

6 HYDRAULIC

syringe taped to wooden arm

parachute

plastic tubing

water

arm

syringe

press

2.5 PARACHUTE RELEASE LEVER

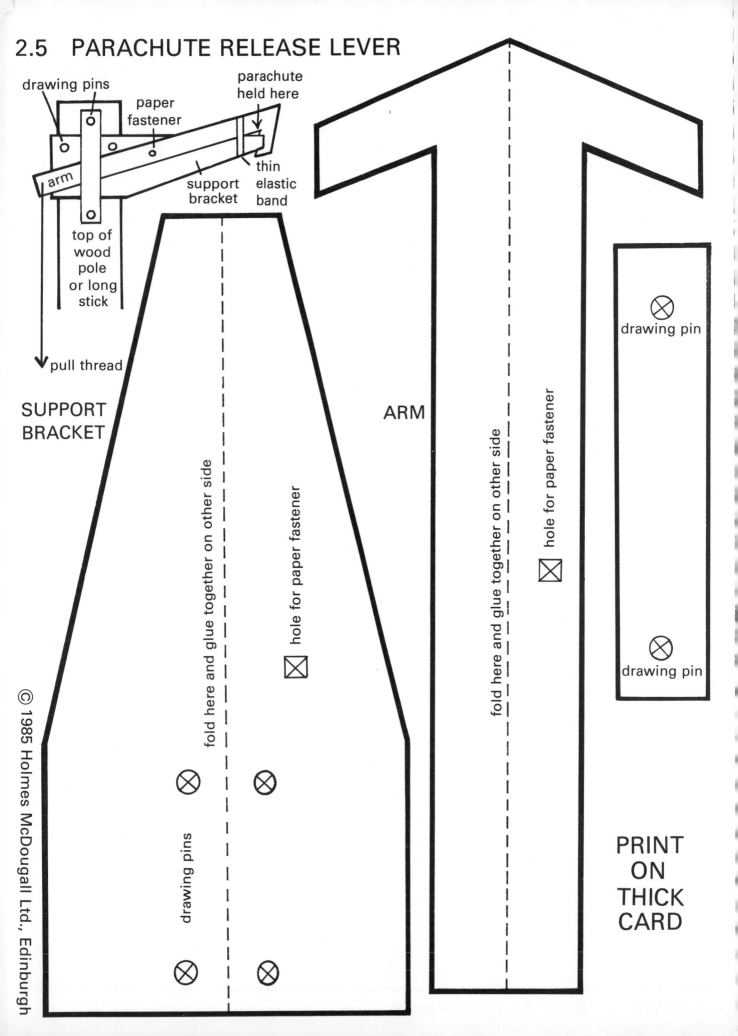

drawing pins

paper fastener

parachute held here

arm

top of wood pole or long stick

pull thread

support bracket

thin elastic band

SUPPORT BRACKET

fold here and glue together on other side

hole for paper fastener

drawing pins

ARM

fold here and glue together on other side

hole for paper fastener

drawing pin

drawing pin

PRINT ON THICK CARD

3.1 ELECTRICAL CONDUCTORS

Scientist _____

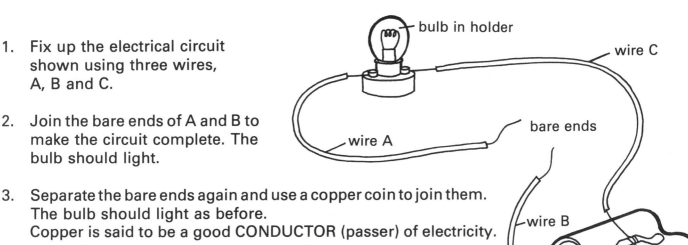

1. Fix up the electrical circuit shown using three wires, A, B and C.

2. Join the bare ends of A and B to make the circuit complete. The bulb should light.

3. Separate the bare ends again and use a copper coin to join them. The bulb should light as before.
   Copper is said to be a good CONDUCTOR (passer) of electricity.

   Use a piece of paper to join the wires, instead of a coin. The bulb does not light.
   Paper is said to be an INSULATOR (non-passer) of electricity.

4. Complete the table below after testing different conductors with your electrical circuit.

ITEM TESTED	DISTANCE	EFFECT ON BULB			CONDUCTS ELECTRICITY		
		bright	dim	out	very well	well	not at all
ALUMINIUM FOIL short piece foil A B	short						
long piece foil A B	long						
IRON WIRE A B short wire	short						
A long wire B	long						
CARBON (pencil lead) A B short piece	short						
pencil cut in half A long piece B	long						
SALTY WATER alter distance B A salty water plastic tub	A & B very close						
	A & B apart						

© 1985 Holmes McDougall Ltd., Edinburgh

3.2 STAGE LIGHTING PROBLEM

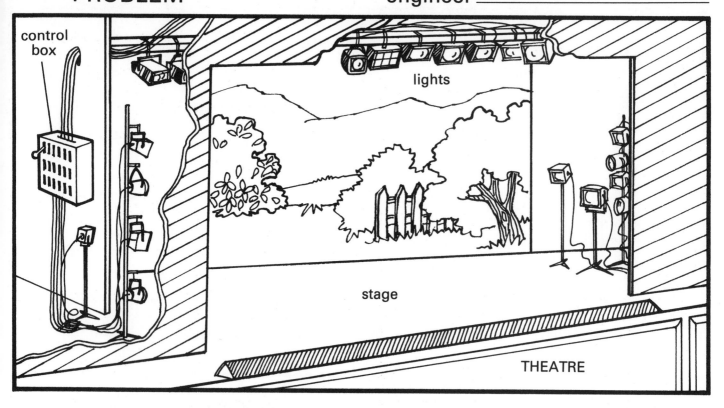

control box

lights

stage

THEATRE

1. If you have been to the theatre, or seen a play on TV, you will know that lighting can be changed to suit the scene — very bright for sunshine, very dim for night time or suspense scenes.

2. You are the engineer who has been asked to fit lighting control switches in a theatre. Your teacher will give you a model theatre with two lights. The bulbs have to be controlled so that you can have both of them very bright, then reduce the brightness until they are both dim.

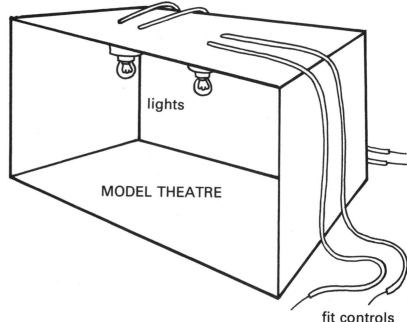

lights

MODEL THEATRE

fit controls to bare ends of wires

3. Fit the dimmer controls outside the box, using any materials you need from the selection available. Ask if you wish to use something which is not supplied. Work out your ideas on a Design Sheet before you start to make your device.

4. Record the results of trials beside each design. Did it work well, poorly, or not at all?

3.3 IDEAS FOR DIMMERS

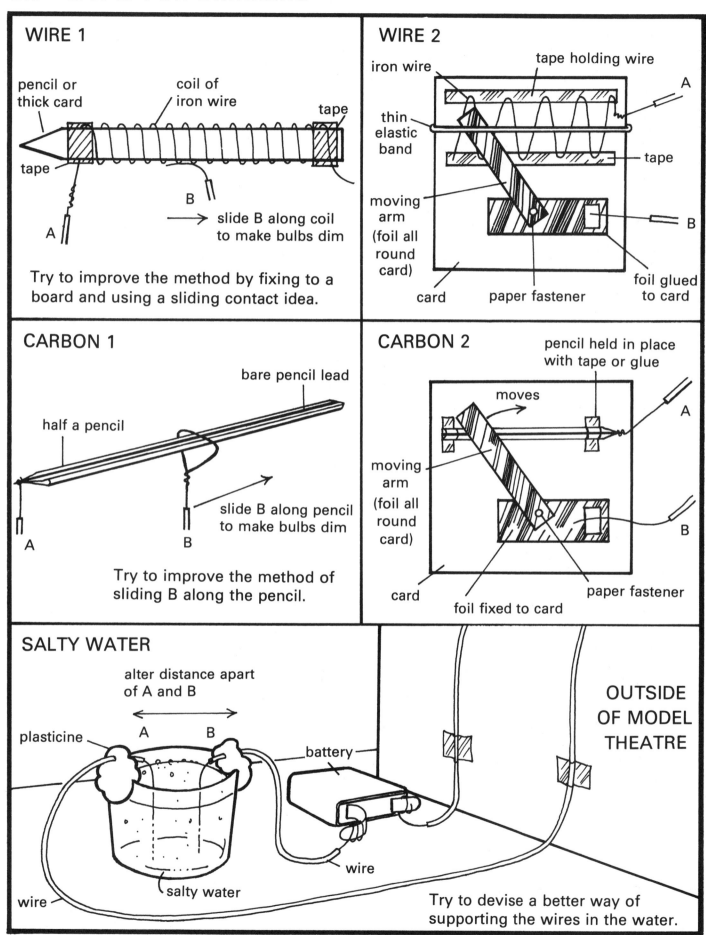

WIRE 1

pencil or thick card

coil of iron wire

tape

tape

A

B

slide B along coil to make bulbs dim

Try to improve the method by fixing to a board and using a sliding contact idea.

WIRE 2

iron wire

tape holding wire

A

thin elastic band

moving arm (foil all round card)

tape

B

card

paper fastener

foil glued to card

CARBON 1

bare pencil lead

half a pencil

slide B along pencil to make bulbs dim

A

B

Try to improve the method of sliding B along the pencil.

CARBON 2

pencil held in place with tape or glue

moves

A

moving arm (foil all round card)

B

card

foil fixed to card

paper fastener

SALTY WATER

alter distance apart of A and B

A   B

plasticine

battery

OUTSIDE OF MODEL THEATRE

wire

salty water

wire

Try to devise a better way of supporting the wires in the water.

1. It is often important to keep a check on the level of
    liquid in a container, such as a petrol tank.

empty | E   ½   F | full
fuel
petrol gauge

2. Make a large water tank from a plastic bottle or ice cream tub, as
    shown. The problem you have to solve is to fix a water level
    warning light to the tank. Your device should switch on a warning
    light when the water reaches the full mark, 5 cm from the top.

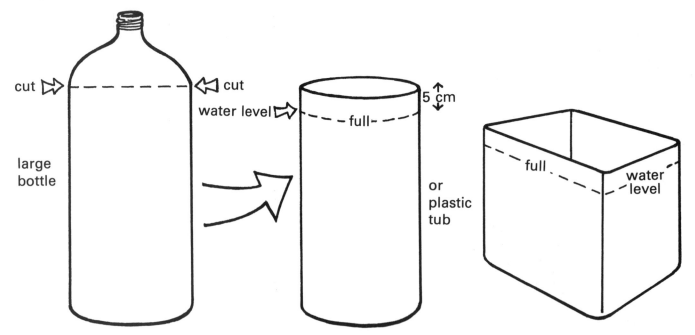

cut ⇨   ⇦ cut
water level ⇨ — full —   5 cm
large
bottle   or
                                    plastic
                                    tub
full   water
          level

3. Think about the problem and look at the selection of materials
    you have been given. Write down your ideas on a Design Sheet,
    with clear labelled drawings. Make a list of any extra things you
    need.

4. Build and test your water level indicator in the tank. Remember to
    empty and refill the tank a few times to make sure that the device
    works well every time the water level rises. Record the test results
    on your Design Sheet.

4.2 IDEAS FOR SWITCHES

1

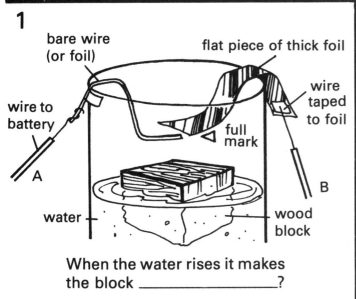

bare wire (or foil)

flat piece of thick foil

wire to battery

wire taped to foil

full mark

A

B

water

wood block

When the water rises it makes the block _____?

2

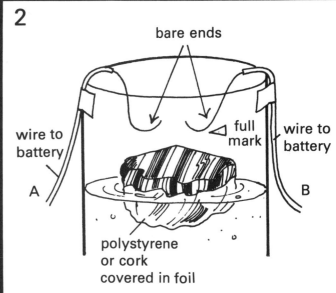

bare ends

wire to battery

full mark

wire to battery

A

B

polystyrene or cork covered in foil

3

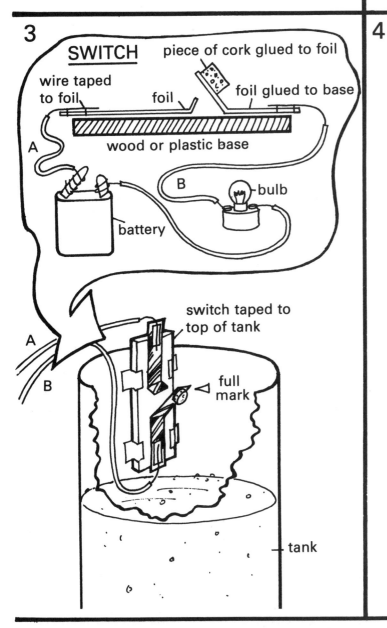

SWITCH

piece of cork glued to foil

wire taped to foil

foil

foil glued to base

wood or plastic base

A

B

bulb

battery

switch taped to top of tank

A

B

full mark

tank

4

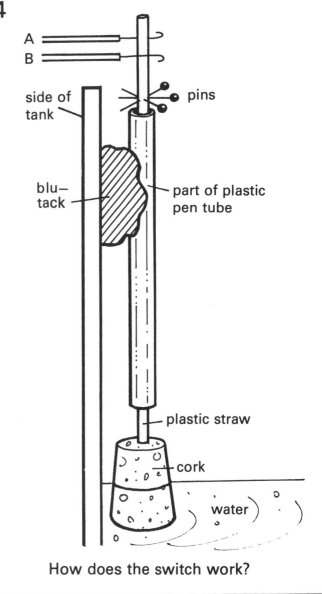

A

B

side of tank

pins

blu-tack

part of plastic pen tube

plastic straw

cork

water

How does the switch work?

5.1 PAWL AND RATCHET

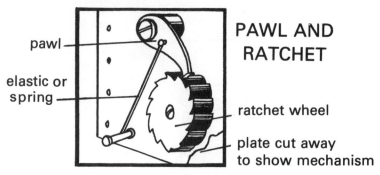

PAWL AND
RATCHET

1. The diagram shows an interesting mechanism which is often used in complicated machines. The PAWL and RATCHET work together in a special way.

2. To find out how this device works, you will need to make a simple model using sheet 5.2 and a piece of wood or cork for a frame. Cut out the parts and assemble them on the frame. The parts should fit neatly over the dotted lines.

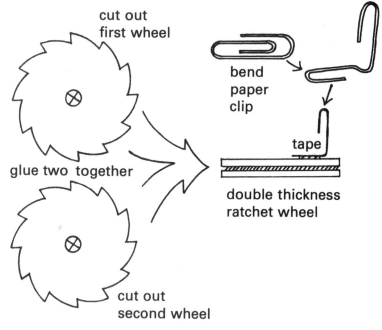

cut out
first wheel

bend
paper
clip

tape

3. Fix a handle to the ratchet wheel, using a bent paper clip as shown.

glue two together

double thickness
ratchet wheel

cut out
second wheel

turn clockwise

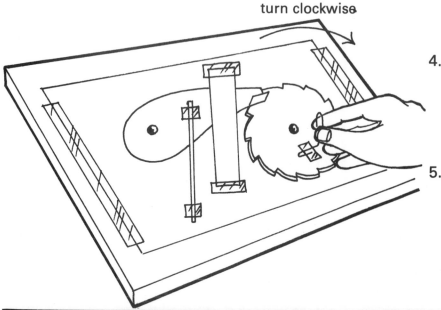

4. Turn the handle of the ratchet wheel *gently* in the direction shown (clockwise = like a clock). Watch what happens. Do this several times.

5. Now try *gently* to turn the wheel in the opposite direction (anti-clockwise). What is happening now? Why do you think this is?

Name _____

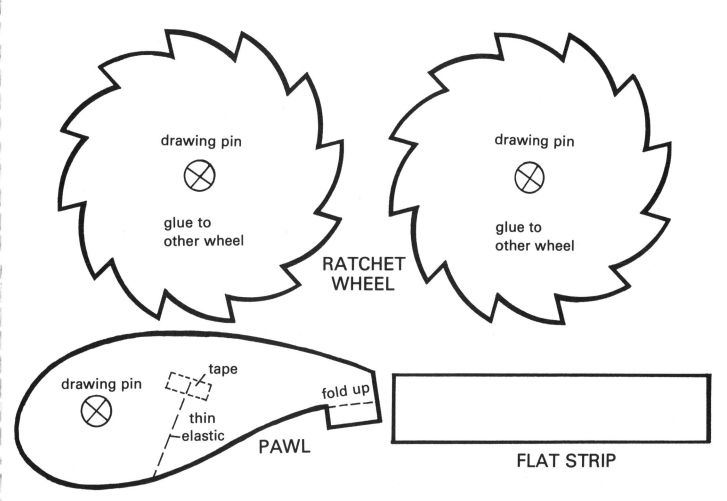

RATCHET WHEEL

drawing pin ⊗

glue to other wheel

drawing pin ⊗

glue to other wheel

PAWL

drawing pin ⊗

tape

thin elastic

fold up

FLAT STRIP

FRAME — glue to wood or cork

tape to frame

flat strip on top of pawl

tape elastic to pawl

drawing pin ⊗

PAWL

FLAT STRIP

thin elastic

tape elastic to frame

tape to frame

drawing pin ⊗

RATCHET WHEEL

PRINT ON THICK CARD

5.3 IDEAS FOR USING PAWL AND RATCHET

1 WEIGHT WINDER

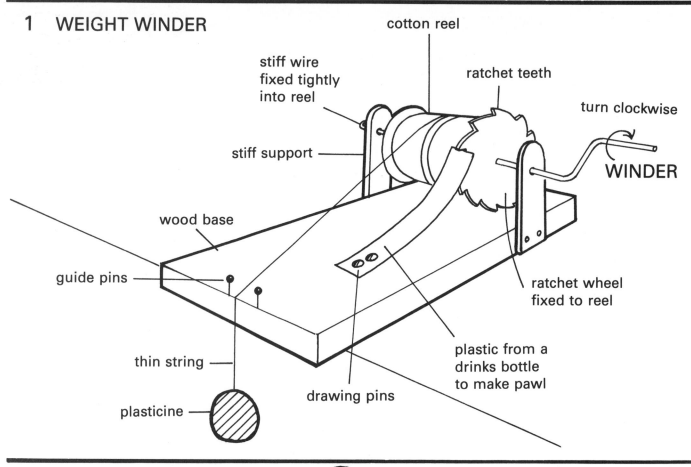

cotton reel

stiff wire fixed tightly into reel

ratchet teeth

turn clockwise

stiff support

WINDER

wood base

ratchet wheel fixed to reel

guide pins

plastic from a drinks bottle to make pawl

thin string

drawing pins

plasticine

2 ONE-WAY TURBINE

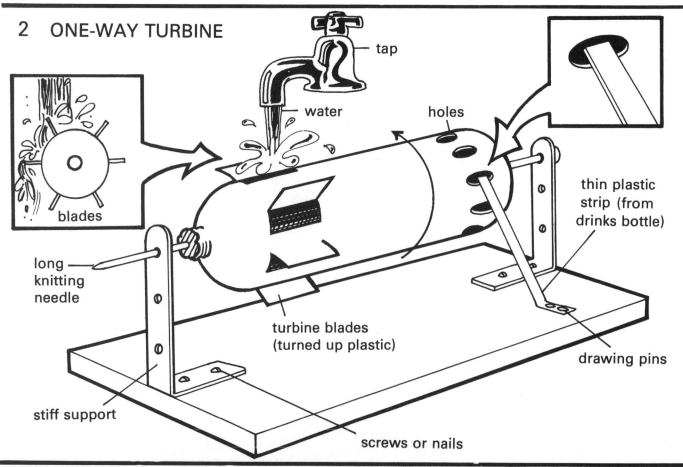

tap

water

holes

blades

thin plastic strip (from drinks bottle)

long knitting needle

turbine blades (turned up plastic)

drawing pins

stiff support

screws or nails

6.1 WHICH KEY?

Security specialist _____

1. Find out which key fits the lock below.

2. You are allowed a pencil, tracing paper and scissors if you need them to make sure that you have found the right key.

3. Put a tick in the correct box when you are certain you are right.

KEY NUMBER	1	2	3	4	5	6	7	8	9	10	11

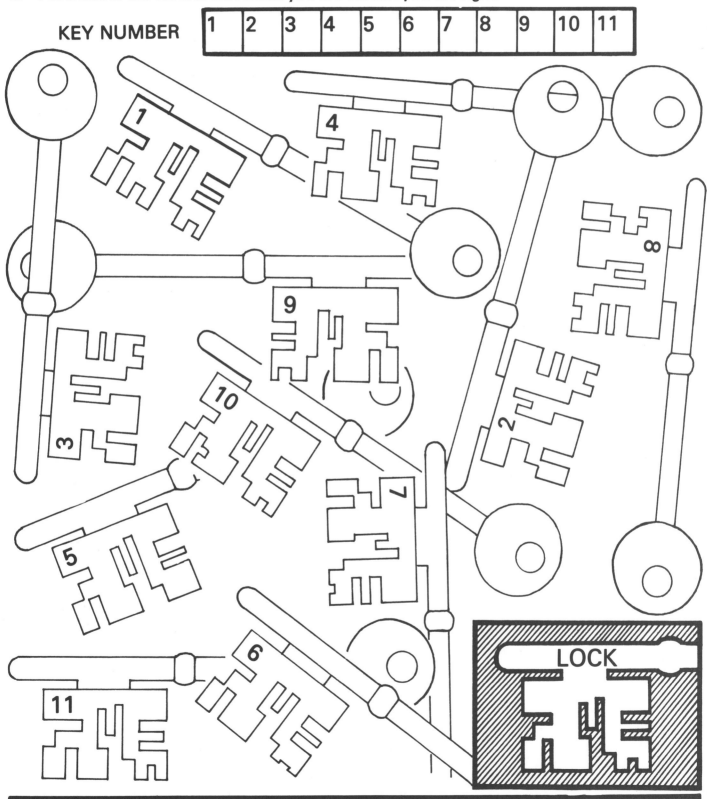

LOCK

6.2 MAKE A KEY CARD

1. **WHAT IS A KEY CARD?**
For electricity to flow a circuit must be complete. The lock shown here is simply a gap in a circuit.
The key is a card with metal foil glued onto it so that it can bridge the gap and complete the circuit.
When the lock gap is bridged by your key card the bulb will light.

bulb in holder
battery
wire
tape
foil   foil
LOCK

2. Cut out a rectangle of card exactly this size.

card
foil
KEY CARD

3. Cut out a strip of aluminium foil and glue it carefully onto your card. Make sure that it is in the right place to make a bridge across the two pieces of foil on the lock.

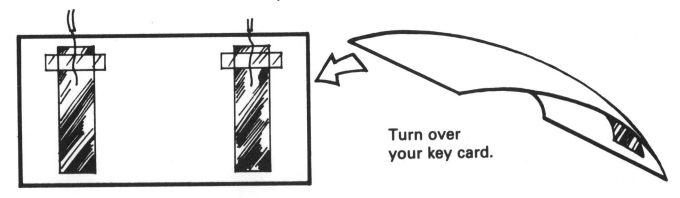

Turn over
your key card.

4. Test your key card on the lock which your teacher will give you. Put the card *face down* on the lock so that the foil bridges the gap in the circuit. Your key card must cover the lock exactly. Now press down firmly and the bulb should light.

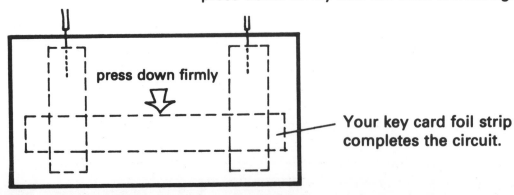

press down firmly

Your key card foil strip completes the circuit.

6.3 WHICH KEY CARD?

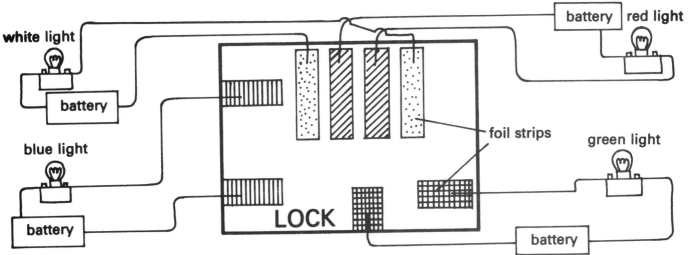

1. This is a more complicated lock. To open it, you have to choose the key card from the four below which will switch on the white light only. The other lights are burglar alarms and *must not light up!*

2. Use a pencil, tracing paper and scissors if you need them to help you find the correct key card. Tick the correct box.

A	B	C	D

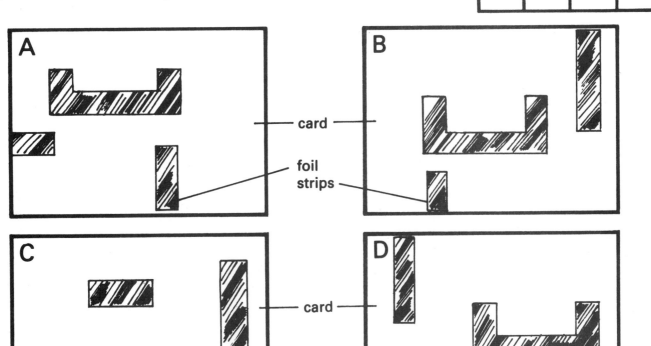

3. Make up the key card which will open this lock and test it on the model lock which your teacher has.

4. Design a card to switch on the red and green lights only. Draw a diagram on a Design Sheet before you try to make the key card.

6.4 BEAT THE BURGLAR!

1. You work for a security firm which has been called in to fit a burglar alarm to a safe containing valuable jewellery. First you need to set up a secure safe, as in the diagram.

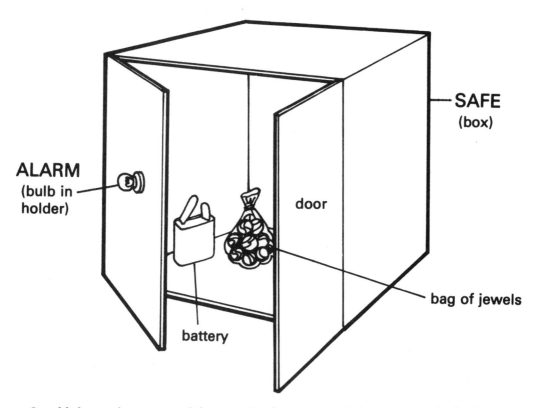

SAFE
(box)

ALARM
(bulb in holder)

door

bag of jewels

battery

2. Using whatever wiring and other materials you need, devise an alarm system to light up the alarm bulb if anyone tries to break into the safe. Plan the alarm on a Design Sheet first, and list the things you will need to make it.

3. Don't forget that *you* must be able to get into the safe without the alarm bulb lighting! Design and make a key to deactivate your alarm.
(KEEP YOUR KEY DESIGN SECRET.)

4. Ask a friend to test how secure your safe is. The only tools the burglar is allowed are a pair of scissors and a piece of card. If the light flashes just once, the burglar has failed to get the bag of jewels.

6.5 IDEAS FOR KEYS AND ALARMS

1

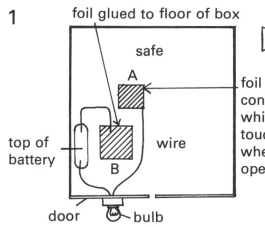

foil glued to floor of box

safe

A

top of battery

wire

B

door — bulb

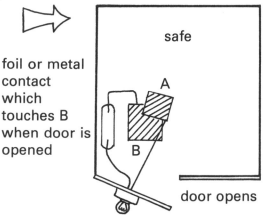

foil or metal contact which touches B when door is opened

safe

A

B

door opens

A & B make contact. The circuit is complete and the bulb lights.

A key for this type of alarm would be a piece of card to slip in between the two contacts A and B, so that the circuit would not be completed on opening the door.

2 TREMBLER ALARMS

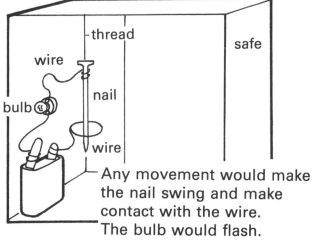

thread

safe

wire

nail

bulb

wire

Any movement would make the nail swing and make contact with the wire. The bulb would flash.

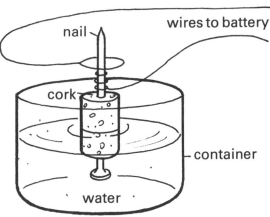

nail

wires to battery

cork

container

water

3 PRESSURE PADS

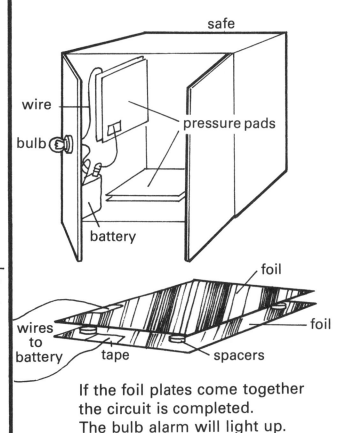

safe

wire

bulb

pressure pads

battery

foil

foil

wires to battery

tape

spacers

If the foil plates come together the circuit is completed. The bulb alarm will light up.

Don't forget that it is possible to wire up a number of these devices to a single alarm bulb.

1. You have a piece of soft iron wire, a paper clip, a pencil, some plasticine and a cardboard box to solve the wire bridge problem!

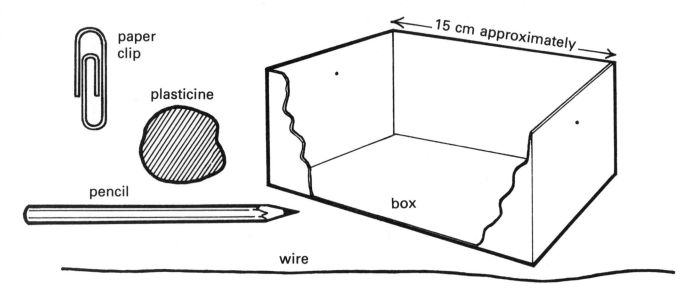

2. Set your bridge up like this. The wire must go through two holes in the sides of the box. The holes must be *exactly* the same height above the table.

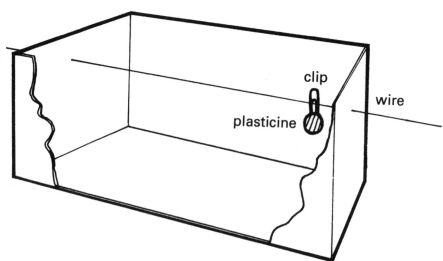

3. Hang the paper clip, weighted with a small piece of plasticine, on one end of the wire. The problem is to make the clip travel to the other side of the box and to come back again, without touching it!

   RULES
   a You are *not* allowed a magnet or anything like that!
   b You are *not* allowed to tilt the box. The two ends of the wire *must* remain level.
   c But — you *are* allowed to move the wire and bend or shape it as you wish.

1. Did you try this?

   Bend the wire and hope that the clip slides down and, when you turn the wire, continues to the other side?

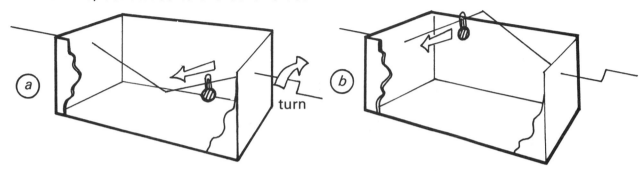

2. Did you try to shake or vibrate the wire and hope to make the clip move across?

3. Did you consider knocking the clip across using bends in the wire?

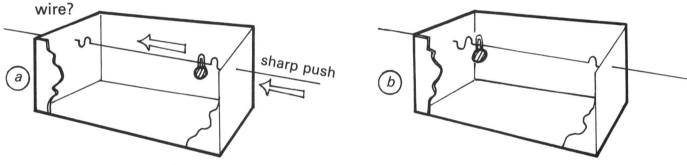

4. A neat solution would be to make a screw from the wire and wind the clip across.
   Try this:

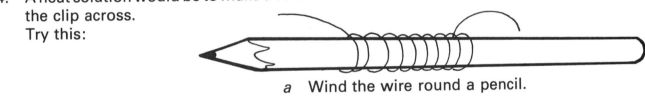

   a Wind the wire round a pencil.

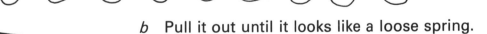

   b Pull it out until it looks like a loose spring.
   c Fit it into the box and attach the paper clip.

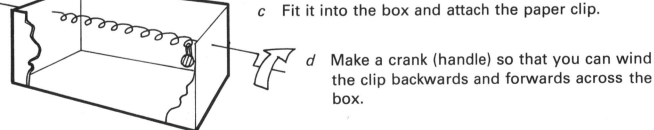

   d Make a crank (handle) so that you can wind the clip backwards and forwards across the box.

5. Can you design a better solution? Draw or write about your ideas on a Design Sheet before you test them.

1. A dispenser is a machine which gives out one item at a time. Your marble dispenser should contain a number of marbles and should release them one at a time as you turn the handle.

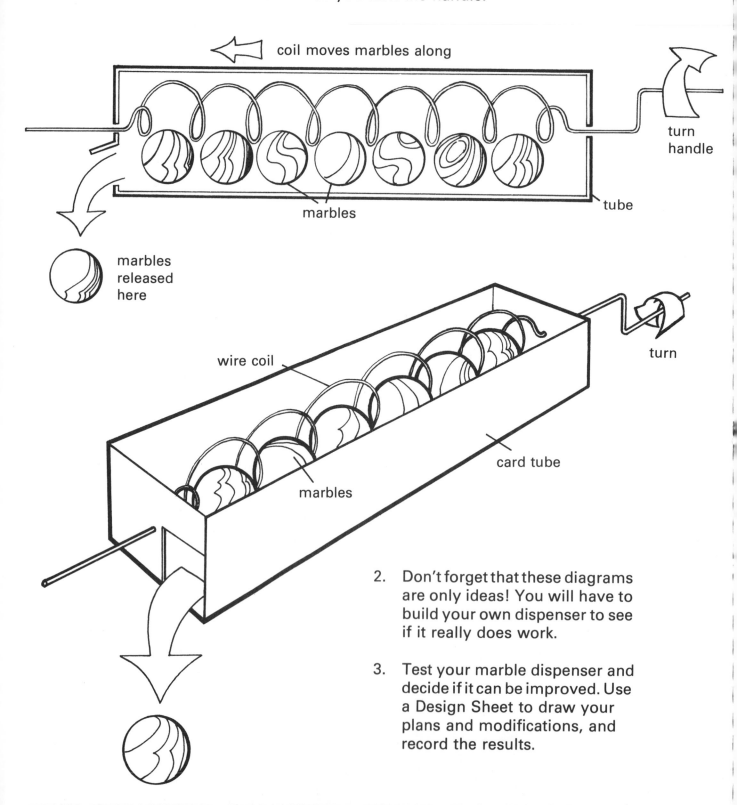

coil moves marbles along

turn handle

marbles

tube

marbles released here

wire coil

card tube

marbles

turn

2. Don't forget that these diagrams are only ideas! You will have to build your own dispenser to see if it really does work.

3. Test your marble dispenser and decide if it can be improved. Use a Design Sheet to draw your plans and modifications, and record the results.

More ideas for a marble dispenser. See if you can improve on them.

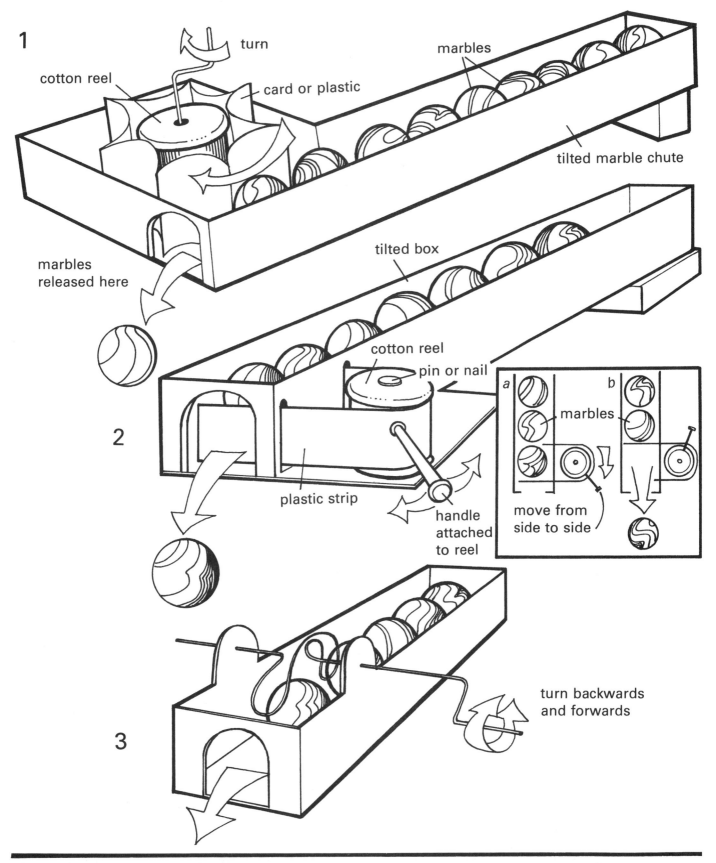

1 turn

cotton reel

card or plastic

marbles

tilted marble chute

marbles released here

tilted box

2

cotton reel

pin or nail

plastic strip

handle attached to reel

a marbles *b*

move from side to side

3

turn backwards and forwards

8.1 MECHANICAL ARMS

Bioengineer _____

1. Cut out the two shapes on sheet 8.2. Pierce holes through X and Y.

2. Attach two strings to A and B. Make them firm with sticky tape.

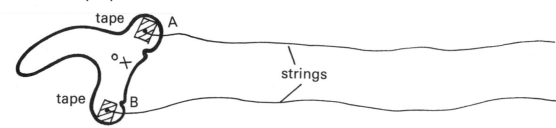

3. Fasten X to Y using a paper fastener.

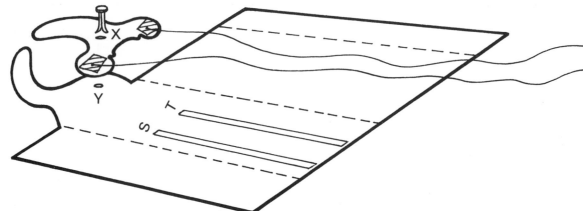

4. Fold the arm along the dotted lines and tape securely, as shown.

5. Glue or tape two straws in position at S and T and thread the strings through them.

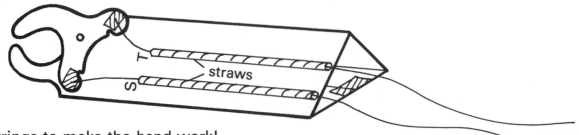

6. Pull the strings to make the hand work!

7. Can you design and build a robot arm with more than two fingers? Draw or write down your ideas on a Design Sheet first.

Bioengineer _____

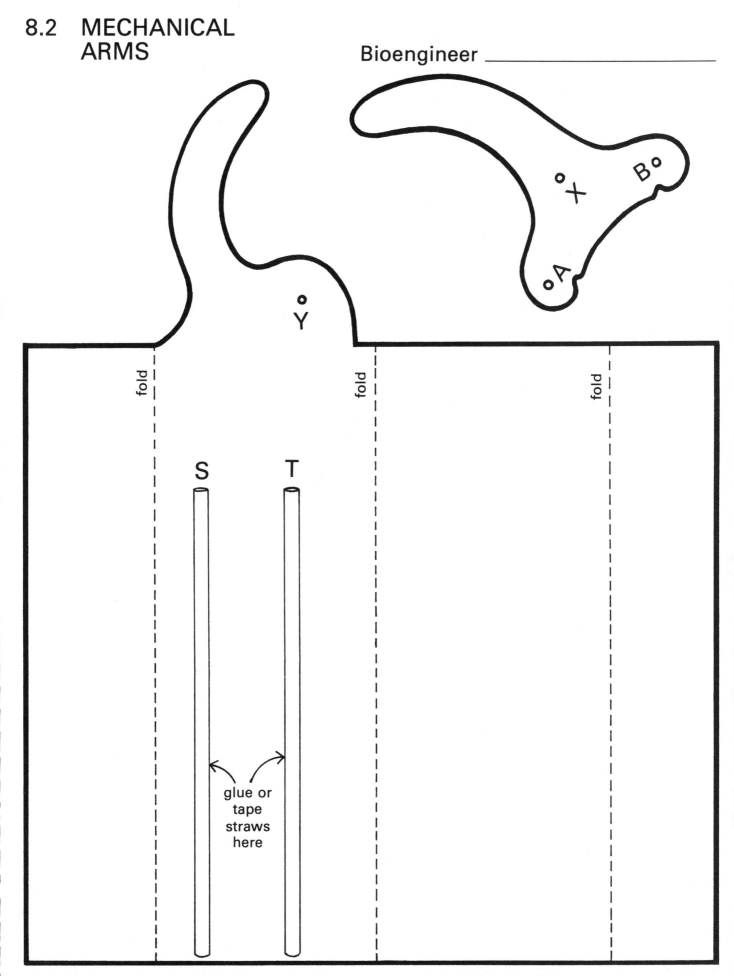

B°

°X

°A

Y°

fold

fold

fold

S

T

glue or
tape
straws
here

PRINT ON THICK CARD

1. The simplest way to build an arm with more than two fingers is to make two X pieces and to add a second Y piece to your mechanical arm.
With two more straws and strings attached you now have four fingers.

   Can you use the arm so that the hand works properly?

   IDEA — tie strings like this so that they work together.

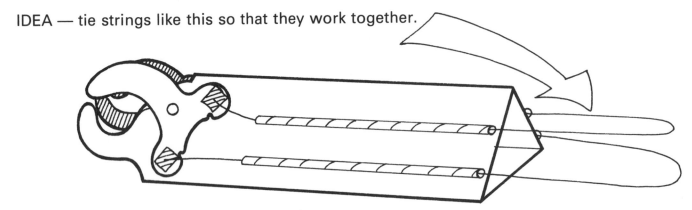

2. Design and test an arm that is as human as possible.

3. Design and test a *jointed* arm.

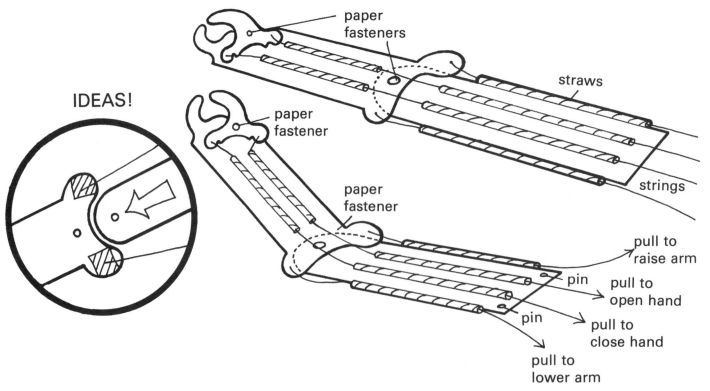

IDEAS!

paper
fasteners

straws

paper
fastener

paper
fastener

strings

pull to
raise arm

pin

pull to
open hand

pin

pull to
close hand

pull to
lower arm

HINT — to get it to work properly, the upper arm must be pinned or taped firmly to a piece of board or a table.

8.4 AN EXTENDING ARM

1. Cut out pieces A B C D E F below and pin them together carefully with paper fasteners.

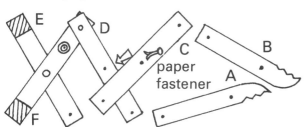

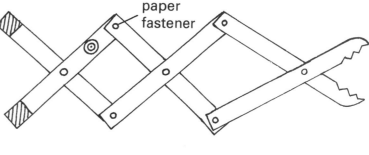

paper fastener

2. Try to solve the problem on sheet 8.5. The drawing pin *must* go through the centre of the Z circle.

paper fasteners here

A

B

C

D

E

Z

F

EMERGENCY NOTICE

EXPLOSION   DANGER!

A CONTAINER HAS TO BE MOVED TO THE SAFETY ZONE!

You may need to design and fit a new small attachment to the pincers at the end of the extending arm.
When you have done this, carefully move the container to the green safety zone.

Signed

URGENT!

PRINT ON THICK CARD

8.5 DANGER — RADIOACTIVE!

Technologist _____

1. Colour the two reaction chambers red and the safety zone green before you start.

2. Pin your extending arm at Z with a drawing pin. Put a second drawing pin upside down in the reaction chamber 309 X.

3. Use the extending arm to move the pin, which is a container of dangerous radioactive material, from 309 X to 4117 Y.

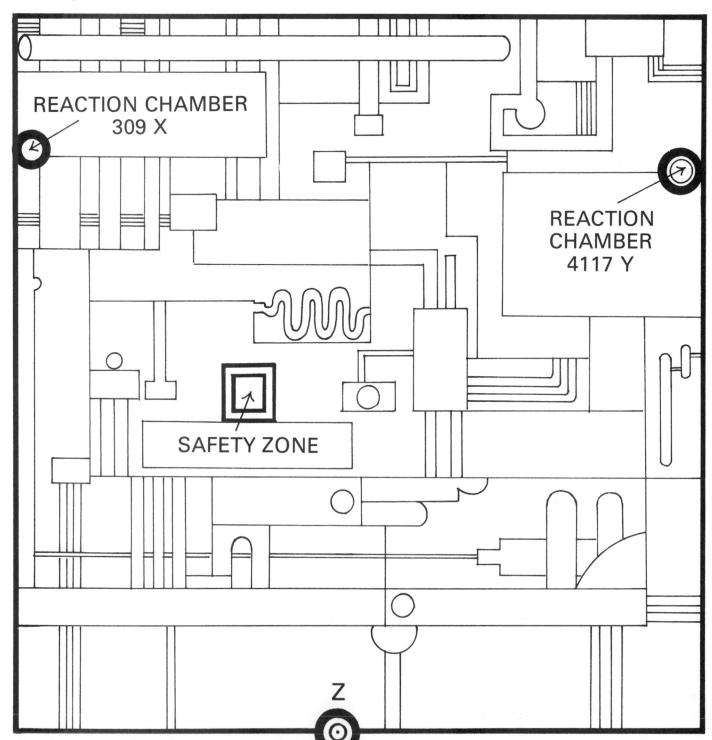

REACTION CHAMBER 309 X

REACTION CHAMBER 4117 Y

SAFETY ZONE

Z

8.6 AN EXTRACTOR

Mechanical engineer

Make and practise using this type of extractor, as follows:

1. Cut a piece of soft iron wire so that it is a little more than twice the length of a plastic straw. Double the wire over as shown.

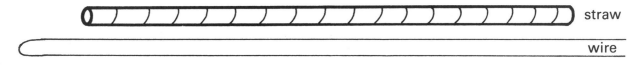

2. Slip the bent wire through the straw.

3. Bend the ends (X and Y) of the wire as shown.

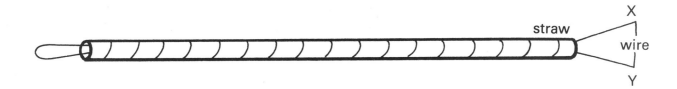

4. Pull the wire loop (Z) gently, and you will find that X and Y are pulled together by the end of your straw.

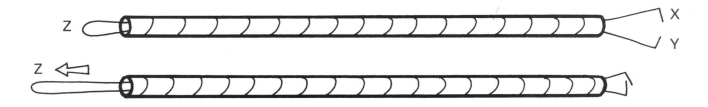

5. To make the extractor stronger and easier to use, tape 'handles' on it, and reinforce the ends of the straw with tape.

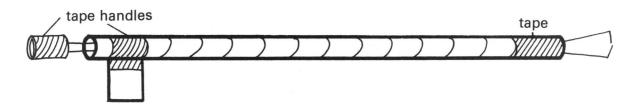

6. Can you devise and make a better extractor? Draw or write about your ideas on a Design Sheet first.

DESIGN SHEET

Design number	Date
Designer	Code

Design title

Technological design group

Category: Open

Classified

Confidential

Secret

Top secret

RESEARCH SHEET

Research topic	Date
	Research team

DATA

TOP SECRET

SCIENCE AND TECHNOLOGY CERTIFICATE

_____

has been awarded this Certificate for

CERTIFICATE OF MERIT

Signed _____

Dated _____

BADGES

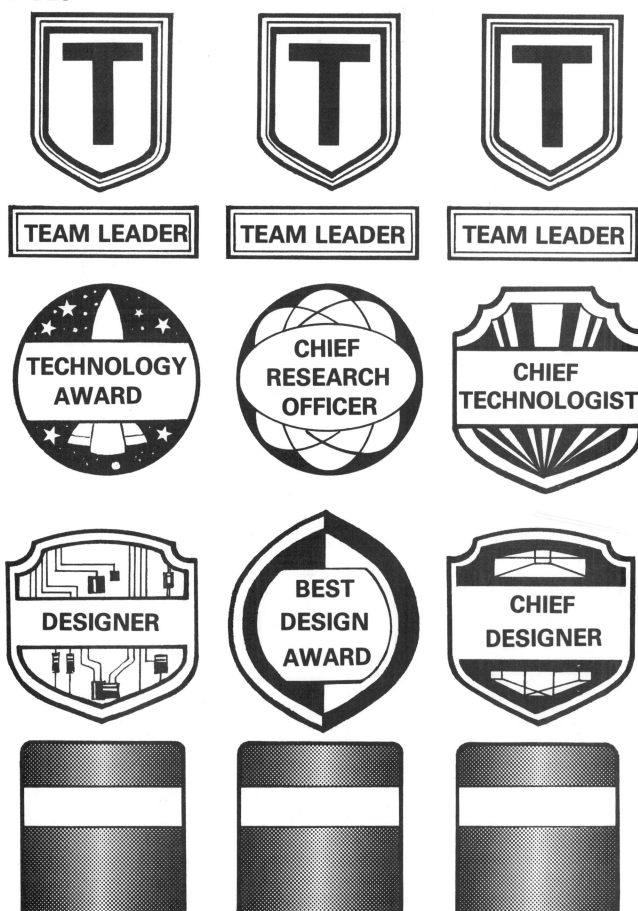

T

T

T

TEAM LEADER

TEAM LEADER

TEAM LEADER

TECHNOLOGY AWARD

CHIEF RESEARCH OFFICER

CHIEF TECHNOLOGIST

DESIGNER

BEST DESIGN AWARD

CHIEF DESIGNER

CLASS RECORDS	Year	1 TEST FLIGHT	2 PARACHUTES	3 ELECTRICITY	4 SENSING DEVICES	5 PAWL AND RATCHET	6 KEYS AND ALARMS	7 ARCHIMEDES SCREW	8 MECHANICAL ARMS
Pupil									